The Episcopal Story

VOLUME 2

in the
**Church's
Teachings
for a
Changing
World**
series

Birth and Rebirth

THOMAS C. FERGUSON

Morehouse Publishing
NEW YORK

Copyright © 2015 by Thomas C. Ferguson

Unless otherwise noted, the Scripture quotations contained herein are from the New Revised Standard Version Bible, copyright © 1989 by the Division of Christian Education of the National Council of Churches of Christ in the U.S.A. Used by permission. All rights reserved.

Morehouse Publishing, 19 East 34th Street, New York, NY 10016

Morehouse Publishing is an imprint of Church Publishing Incorporated.
www.churchpublishing.org

Cover art: *Angels* by Kathy Eppick
Cover design by Laurie Klein Westhafer
Interior design and typesetting by Beth Oberholtzer Design

Library of Congress Cataloging-in-Publication Data

Ferguson, Thomas C.
    The Episcopal story : birth and rebirth / Thomas C. Ferguson.
        pages cm. — (The church's teachings for a changing world series ; Volume 2)
    ISBN 978-0-8192-3221-2 (pbk.) — ISBN 978-0-8192-3222-9 (ebook)
1. Church history. 2. Episcopal Church—History. 3. Anglican Communion—History. I. Title.
    BR145.3.F48   2015
    283'.7309—dc23

                                                                2015022380

Printed in the United States of America

Contents

Introduction

A clergy colleague and I were once talking, yes, bemoaning the state of the church. When he sighed and said, "Oh well, the church has always changed slowly, so I guess there's no use complaining," I almost spat out my coffee. He looked at me, startled, and I said, "Well, actually, the church has changed dramatically any number of times, often in ways no one could have seen, in as short as a generation."

A Christian born around the year 300, who would have grown up when Christians were a small minority suffering under the most systematic persecution ever attempted, may have lived to see Christianity become the official religion of the Roman Empire by 379. For someone born in 1760 in America, the Anglican Church in America had become the Episcopal Church by 1810. Far from the Church never changing, or changing slowly, there's example after example to prove the opposite is true. Adaptation is sometimes a long, drawn-out, centuries-long process. Sometimes it happens fast, because of events and developments thrust onto the Church and world.

The title of this book—*The Episcopal Story: Birth and Rebirth*—is my effort to capture this truth, that the Church has always been involved in a dynamic process of evolution, adaptation, and change. This theme stands in contrast to some perceived understandings of how Christianity has developed. I have seen these as

- a linear model,
- a cyclical model, and
- a decline-and-fall model.

Linear Model

Lecturing on the history of Lutheranism, a colleague demonstrated what I think of as the linear model using a poster (cast your mind back to those days before PowerPoint). On it was the church as the trunk of a tree, beginning with Jesus and the apostles, with various branches snaking out from that central trunk. The thickest branch was the early, apostolic church; other branches indicated the division between Eastern and Western Christianity. More branches represented the differing expressions of Christianity that broke from the Roman Catholic Church during the sixteenth-century Reformation; and so on. At the top, the very highest branch, was Lutheranism, as the most complete manifestation of the gospel.

Eventually, the poster started to wear out, so he ordered another. Later, he was giving the same talk, and turned to the poster—and discovered, with some alarm, that at the top was not the Lutheran Church, but the Presbyterians. He called the company that produced the poster and learned that they printed several versions, with different churches at the top. When he told me this story, we had a vision of Presbyterians, Methodists, Baptists, and Episcopalians giving the same talk, pointing at their poster, confident that their expression of Christianity was the most highly evolved form of Christianity.

That's a linear understanding of church history: a progression from point A to Z, more often than not with Z being one's brand of Christianity as the pinnacle. This book is not a history of the Episcopal Church as the end-point of a logical and divine progression of Christianity.

Cyclical Model

A cyclical view is, in some ways, the exact opposite of the linear. Rather than a clear progression toward some high point, the story of Christianity is one of the same issues coming up again and again. We can see an example of this in some understandings of Pentecostalism: they would say the story of Christianity is one of the cyclical in-breaking of the Holy Spirit, whether it be the Montanist Movement in the third century or Spiritual Franciscans in the fourteenth century or the birth of modern Pentecostal movements in the twentieth century.

If you put too much emphasis on cycles, however, you may discount the significance of context. The situation of third century Asia Minor that shaped the Montanist movement is very, very different from Los Angeles in 1906, when Pentecostalism as we know it today was born. Hunting for cyclical models can also be a way to privilege what we consider essential. While Pentecostals might choose the in-breaking of the Holy Spirit, the Roman Catholic Church might prioritize understanding of the authority of the bishop of Rome. Often the issues we identify as essential to the cyclical cycles happen to be our own sacred cows.

Decline and Fall Model

This model picks a moment when Christianity went "bad." Different Christian groups may isolate instances of "decline," as some Catholics think the reform spirit of the Second Vatican Council marked the end of true Roman Catholicism. Some Episcopalians are convinced the Church declined because of the ordination of women in the 1970s. It's not that there aren't significant moments of transition in Christianity. It's that singling out particular ones as somehow definitive often tells us more about our current day—or a particular group's dissatisfaction with the Church—than it does about the past.

Having outlined and discounted these three models, it may seem audacious to introduce one of my own. I do so, however, fully acknowledging its limitations, but also realizing that it helps to identify overarching themes when you're covering the history of Christianity from the time of Jesus to the present, with particular emphasis on the development of Anglicanism and the Episcopal Church. In this humble effort, I will focus on three core themes.

One is **diversity**. Christianity has always—always—been a diverse movement, even in the sepia-toned, mythologized "early church" of the first few centuries. There was never a time when Christianity was not diverse.

A second theme is **adaptation**. Christianity goes through a repeated process of being formed and shaped by a particular context, only to see that context change. Christianity was born in the Jewish context of the Roman province of Judea, but almost immediately went through a process of adaptation to a largely non-Jewish context. When the predominant context for Christianity changes, Christianity changes. This is as true for the twentieth century as it was in the sixteenth century.

A third is **globalization**. Christianity has always been a global religion, though the understanding of what the "globe" meant has changed throughout time. There is evidence of a Christian presence in India perhaps by the year 100, and what is now Ethiopia by the year 300. Similarly, there were significant Christian populations outside the boundaries of the Roman Empire by the year 400. By 700, there were Christian missionaries in China. We are living in yet another profound phase of globalization of Christianity, with significant increase in numbers and influence of Christians living in Africa, Asia, and South America. If anyone in Europe and North America thinks of Christianity as a "Western" phenomenon, they need to think again. Christianity has always been a globalized movement, and as both Anglicanism and the Episcopal Church become more global, they are living into one of the most essential elements of the Christian story.

These organizing themes are in no way intended to be exhaustive, and I readily admit they likely have their own weaknesses. I offer them and the conversation that follows, hoping to build bridges and connections across different eras and to illuminate the Episcopal Story in the context of the longer, fuller Christian story.

In Gratitude

In order to be a teacher, one must first have been taught. I am particularly thankful to the mentors who have nurtured me over the years, in particular Ron Cameron and Rabbi Roger Klein at Wesleyan University, Rowan Greer at Yale Divinity School, and especially Rebecca Lyman from the Church Divinity School of the Pacific/Graduate Theological Union. I also want to remember my late grandmother, Evelyn Vradenburgh, who taught me the most about what it meant to be both a Christian and a teacher. I am indebted to Stephanie Spellers, not only for inviting me to contribute to the series *Church's Teaching for a Changing World*, but also for the passion, vision, and energy she has brought to this project as my primary editor. Finally, I would like to thank my wife and son, who have shown tremendous patience through the years with my outbursts at the historical inaccuracies of period dramas and History Channel specials.

And so we begin where the study of the history of Christianity almost always does: with Jesus and the birth of the church.

Part I

Chapter 1

Jesus and the Birth of Christianity

I was once asked to guest lecture on "Judaism in the Time of Jesus," and I had to reply, "Only if I get to rename the lecture 'Judaism**S** in the time of Jesus.'" The life and teachings of Jesus need to be set against the backdrop of the Judaisms of his time, keeping in mind that Judaism was far from a monolith.

Judaisms in the Time of Jesus

Within the diversity of Judaisms of Jesus's time, all Jews likely would have agreed on three important elements:

- **The centrality of the Jewish Temple**. Most Jews defined themselves either by their adherence to the Temple and its elaborate set of liturgies or by their explicit rejection of the Temple as having been corrupted. It was the home of the Ark of the Covenant containing the Law, and on the holiest of days, Yom Kippur, the High Priest made atonement there for the sins of the people. The current Western (or Wailing) Wall in Jerusalem is but a small fragment, a lower structural retaining wall, of the massive, gold-covered, awe-inspiring Temple.

- **The Law of Moses, or Torah**. Alongside the Temple, the first five books of the Hebrew Bible defined life for Jews. Many Jews also held to an oral law or set of traditions handed down with the books of the Law. For the Jewish people, who believed they were in a special covenant relationship with God, the Law was the means by which God's will was recognized and fulfilled.

Figure 1 Map of Judea in the time of Jesus.

- **The growing place of the synagogue**. The synagogue was both the local site where the Torah was read and the occasional sermon preached, and a sort of local meeting house/community center for Jewish communities. It was particularly important in Galilee, north of Jerusalem, where Jesus operated and often taught. The synagogue gained increasing importance for Jewish communities scattered throughout the Empire.

Judaism had its fair share of groupings and divisions in Jesus's time. The most well known historian of the period, Josephus (died around 100 CE), famously listed three different groups: Sadducees, Pharisees, and Essenes. The **Sadducees** focused on Jerusalem, the Temple, and religious observance. The **Pharisees** were their polar opposite: centered in Galilee, north of Jerusalem, they attended to Torah study and the local synagogue. The biblical Gospels speak often of Jesus's negative interactions with the Pharisees, but let the reader beware. Given that there was quite likely some conflict between Jesus's followers and Pharisees, reconstructing an image of them from the Gospels would be like reconstructing an image of the British from American sources from the Revolutionary War. Josephus also listed the **Essenes**, a catch-all term for ascetic, almost quasi-monastic expressions of Judaism. Later scholars have argued that the community responsible for the Dead Sea Scrolls were related to the Essenes.

Josephus's tidy threefold division doesn't capture the true range of Judaisms in Jesus's day. The foremost example is John the Baptizer, a charismatic teacher who gathered a group of followers and preached a message of repentance. The New Testament also mentions groups like lawyers and scribes, as well as zealots who advocated for liberation from the Roman Empire.

There was also a significant **Jewish diaspora**, or those Jews who lived in other parts of the world. Estimates are tough to come by, but it seems the Jewish population of the Roman Empire was likely between 5 and 10 percent. The Jewish community in the

Figure 2 The War Scroll from the Dead Sea scrolls, describing the war between the sons of light and sons of darkness.

city of Alexandria in Egypt was large enough to merit their own quarter of the city. Jewish communities spread even further afield, into the cities of the Persian Empire and as far away as what is now Ethiopia.

It's one thing to note that Jesus's ministry of preaching and teaching was grounded in a Jewish context: it's another thing to appreciate the complexity and diversity of that context.

Political Context

Jesus and his followers were surrounded by intense political ferment. The geographic entity we now see on a map as Israel was, in Jesus's time, several different political and cultural entities. The Jewish people sat at the crossroads of the great empires of the ancient world, ruled at various times by Egyptians, Assyrians, Persians, Greeks, and Medes, just to name a few. They also periodically enjoyed independence and self-rule. Just before the time of Jesus, the Jewish people once again enjoyed a period of independence, following a successful revolt against the Syrian kings. Eventually, though, the Jewish people succumbed to Roman rule like much of what we now call the Middle East.

The **Romans** often preferred to rule indirectly through locals rather than get overly involved in regional matters. So the Romans set up a local king who managed day-to-day affairs but was responsible for sending taxes to Rome: **King Herod**, who ruled from 37 BCE to 4 BCE. At the time of Jesus, the territory of King Herod had been divided up. **Herod Antipas**, one of Herod's descendants, ruled Jesus's hometown of Galilee. Rome took direct control of the southern region around Jerusalem, called Judaea, appointing a series of governors, the most well known being **Pontius Pilate**, governor from 26 to 36 CE. So long as the taxes were paid and order kept, tolerance was the norm. Rome could, however, come down swiftly and forcefully if the authorities feared disturbance would result.

Given the diversity and geographic expansion of the empire, Roman culture served as the glue among a disparate people. Many subjects adopted the toga, honored Roman civic offices and organization, and participated in "emperor worship." This may seem blasphemous today, but you could think of emperor worship as an ancient version of pledging allegiance to the flag: the emperor was a symbol of unity, so people paid homage to him by burning a candle in front of his statue or pouring out a glass of wine in libation.

The Ministry and Teaching of Jesus

It was into this diverse, dynamic political and religious background that Jesus of Nazareth emerged. On the one hand, he was one of many teachers and preachers on the scene. On the other hand, he hardly fit into anyone's mold or expectation, certainly not for a Messsiah, Son of Man or savior of the Jewish people. Some significant aspects of Jesus's ministry included:

- **His radical ethics based on the Law of Moses**. As Jesus said, he did not come to abolish the Law but to fulfill it (Matthew 5:17). If anything, he extended beyond the Sadducees and Pharisees in his application of the Law. Where the Law forbade adultery, Jesus said avoid even lust. Yet he reversed course to ignore elements of the Law that hindered true faithfulness or had become ends of themselves (such as some rules about washing and fasting). Jesus's shorthand description of this ethical teaching was "the kingdom of God," or "reign of God," a society reshaped in accordance with God's vision of justice and wholeness.

- **The apocalyptic element in his teaching**. Jesus believed God would intervene and restore the proper ordering of the world, but he warned that the period after his death and before the second coming would be a time of urgency for the spread of the message. Early Christianity was immersed in this tension and urgency.

- **His understanding of community**. Jesus often spoke directly to the Jewish people, to call them back to the covenant with God. But his sense of community stretched well beyond those bounds. He traveled outside of the land of Israel to preach; he included those traditionally marginalized by society, such as tax collectors and women, among his disciples; and he charged his disciples with gathering followers from every tribe and land to make one community.

Early Spread of Christianity

The Roman state executed Jesus around the year 29. The method was crucifixion, a penalty reserved for rebels and the lowest of criminals. His crime? He was considered a threat to the civil order. Many were unhappy with Jesus and his teachings, but it's tough to tell who brought and really pushed those charges. There is a trajectory from the earliest Gospel (Mark) to the latest (John) to shift the blame increasingly from the Romans to the Jews. In Mark, it is a small, unnamed group of Jewish leaders; by the Gospel of John, Jesus's enemies are grouped under the inchoate and all-encompassing term "the Jews."

After Jesus's death, his followers came to believe he had been raised from the dead. The earliest Gospel, Mark, ends with an empty tomb, but stories of Jesus's post-resurrection appearances abound. Empowered by the belief that Jesus had been raised, the disciples continued to spread the message not only of Jesus's ethical and spiritual teachings, but of him as the risen Son of God, the vindicated righteous one. Here are just a few highlights about those early communities:

- **Jerusalem and the Temple**. Jesus's followers still went to the Temple and still observed the Jewish Law. Tensions occasionally erupted between disciples and other Jews in Jerusalem. James, who is called the "brother of the Lord," led the Jerusalem community until his martyrdom.

- **Pauline mission**. Saul of Tarsus, later to take the name Paul, was instrumental in helping spread Christianity from its Jewish base into the Gentile (or non-Jewish) milieu of the empire. Paul was steeped in Jewish law, having been a Pharisee. However he added an important element to Jesus's proclamation: The notion of the New Covenant mediated by Jesus that replaced the old Jewish law. In Jesus and in baptism, Paul said, there is a new creation (2 Corinthians 5:17). Therefore the old Jewish law no longer applied the same way, and Gentiles could be equal and full members of the community (Ephesians 2:11–22). It's not difficult to imagine the ensuing tension between groups inspired by Paul and those who sought continuity with the practices of Judaism.

Even in this short chapter, you can see the emergence of the organizing themes: the broad diversity of beliefs and expressions, the ways Jews and early Christians adapted to the Roman world, and the influence of global perspectives on Jewish and early Christian life. All these elements continue to shape the story and the faith as they spread further.

Chapter 2

Globalization 1.0:
Christianity Goes Global

Over a decade ago my wife and I were in the city of Palermo on Sicily. It was a beautiful day, so we decided to walk from one of the local attractions back to our hotel. We got hopelessly lost and found ourselves wandering through twisting and turning streets, walking down dead-end alleyways and eventually losing our sense of direction entirely. Then we turned a corner and saw a four-lane road, running straight as an arrow. I said to my wife, "This must have been built by the Romans."

Romans were great road-builders, mostly because they had to move legions about the Empire and carry communication and trade by land. While not as networked as our current world, Christianity had the good fortune to be birthed when the ancient world was about as connected as it could be. These roads, postal networks, and trade contacts helped Christianity to take hold in the great urban centers of the ancient world—so much so that for several hundred years Christianity was seen as an urban faith, like we might consider good zydeco music a New Orleans phenomenon.

As it spread from its predominantly Jewish context, Christianity had to adapt profoundly to that globalized, networked ancient Roman world.

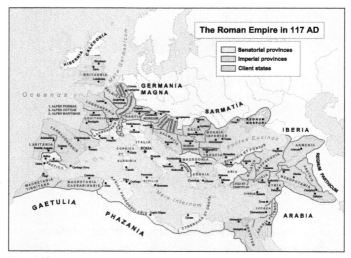

Figure 3 The Roman Empire at its greatest extent under Emperor Trajan, circa 100.

Relationship with Judaism: Some Explaining to Do

Before beginning its spread through the ancient world, Christianity had to figure out whether it was a form of Judaism or not. Did someone have to become a Jew in order to become a follower of Jesus? In the ancient world, this meant adopting the requirements of the Law of Moses, including circumcision, limiting one's contact with non-Jews in certain cases, and following dietary restrictions. The issue came to a head in the first generation of Jesus's followers, with the apostles Peter and Paul leading separate camps. As described in the Book of Acts, the **apostle Paul** asked for a summit in Jerusalem to hash the issue out. They agreed converts need not be circumcised, though they upheld some aspects of Jewish law, like avoiding meat sacrificed during the worship of Greek gods in temples. This decision released Christianity to make inroads among non-Jews for whom things like circumcision or limiting contact with non-Jews would have been a bar too high.

Political developments also shaped the new movement's relationship to its Jewish forebears. In the years 66–70, Jews in what we now call Israel rebelled against Roman rule. After initial victories, they lost the war and suffered a devastating defeat, culminating in the year 70 with the **destruction of the Temple** in Jerusalem. Christians fled Jerusalem during the war and began to interpret the destruction of the Temple as a sign of God's punishment. They claimed Jesus's followers were now the true chosen people and heirs of God's covenant. That said, well into the 400s, Christian preachers were still exhorting believers not to go to the synagogue or observe Jewish customs, the best proof that significant interaction between Jews and Christians continued for quite some time in some areas.

Judaism certainly didn't sit still during this period. Without the Temple as a central focus, Jews began to reshape the faith around the rabbis and the synagogue. Instead of the elaborate set of Temple rituals, the emphasis shifted to interpretation of the Law of Moses and living it out in daily life—a movement that became rabbinic Judaism as we now know it.

A Peculiar People

Christianity traveled throughout the empire, facilitated by the relative ease of travel and networks of personal connection. Those networks also tended to encompass a broad social strata. While some religions appealed to narrow segments of society, Christians preached that baptism made everyone more or less equal, and in the highly social- and class-stratified Roman world, slaves and the wealthy worshipped alongside one another (though there was plenty of tension between rich and poor).

People recognized Christians as a close-knit community that cared for one another. They took in widows and orphans. They collected money to distribute to the poor. Christians came to be seen as unusual and distinctive, and for everyone who thought Christians strange, others were curious and drawn.

Learning to Speak Greek

As Christianity spread throughout the empire, it attracted more and more non-Jewish converts. As it did so, Christianity needed to figure out how to express itself in a culturally different milieu than its original Jewish context. The predominant culture of the eastern half of the Roman Empire, where Christianity first began

Figure 4 Icon of Justin Martyr (d. circa 165), showing him wearing the distinctive philosopher's robe.

to spread, was Greek. A simple form of Greek, called koine or "common" Greek, was the language of commerce and culture, just as you're likely to see menu items in English when you go to a restaurant in Prague or Beijing. Christianity needed to learn how to speak Greek.

How would Christians take a message formed in an originally Jewish context and make it sensible to a predominantly Greek culture? Some words had to be swapped out altogether: *Christos* might have meant someone anointed and set apart by God to Hebrew speakers, but Greeks might have asked, "Is your God an athlete?" (since athletes were covered with oil before a competition).

Other translation depended on linking Christian thought with philosophy on the ground. Prominent convert and former philosopher **Justin Martyr** (d. 165) taught in Rome and made the link between Jesus—the "Logos"—and Greek philosophy. He leaned on Plato, who spoke of a distant, hopelessly removed creator God, a "first principle," and a sort of lesser divine being who formed the world out of preexisting matter left lying around by the creator, the "second principle." It wasn't such a stretch: the Book of Proverbs (8:22) notes that "God created wisdom [*or "logos" in Greek*] as the beginning of all his works." The Gospel of John starts with "in the beginning was The Word." Adapting elements of Greek philosophy like this helped non-Jewish converts to come on board, and became central to the development of the Christian story.

Formation of Communities

In the first and second centuries, the diversity of Christian community was nearly mind-boggling. There was no centralized authority to define what was "right" or "wrong." There was no complete, agreed-upon list of books of the Bible: some communities were devoted to certain books that we've never seen as part of an "official" canon. Some groups even rejected the idea that the God of the Jews was the same as the God of Jesus, and they refused to read the Hebrew Bible in their worship. Some groups, now referred to as Gnostics, believed Jesus came to reveal a special and secret truth as opposed to Christians who believed salvation was offered to all who believed and were baptized.

Slowly, gradually, painfully, a consensus began to emerge, with three components:

1. The formation of statements of belief, which came to be known as **creeds**
2. The effort to agree on authoritative books, the start of forming a **canon** of Scripture
3. A succession of teaching authority in the church, which coalesced around the office of **bishop**

We see an example of these three elements in the life and teaching of **Irenaeus**, bishop of Lyons in what is now Southern France. He spoke of a "rule of truth," a very rudimentary Creed. Against the Gnostic understanding of "secret" teaching revealed in their books, he claimed texts used by "catholic" Christians were more authoritative (or canonical) than the Gnostic texts, because they had been in circulation longer and were connected to prominent apostles. And he traced a succession of teaching in the office of bishop: he learned from Polycarp, who learned from John the Apostle, who learned from Jesus. There was no true centralized authority, but as the second century progressed, the pressure mounted to nail down the essentials of what it meant to be "Christian."

Figure 5   Just some of the dozens of texts found in the Nag Hammadi library. Note that these are codices/books instead of scrolls.

Pushback

As it spread, Christianity came into conflict with the Roman world. But how much of the mythologization around **Christian persecution** is fact? On the one hand, when persecution took place, it was quite often shocking and brutal. On the other hand, prior to the mid-third century, persecution of Christians was sporadic and usually initiated by local circumstances. For many years and in many places, Christians worshipped more or less freely.

Why did conflict arise? Why were authorities so nervous about Christians?

- **They were separate**. Christians consciously set themselves apart from the society around them. They refused to participate in ritual acts associated with the emperor, which must have looked like refusing to pledge allegiance to the flag. And while Jews were excused because they were considered an ancient religion, Romans viewed Christianity as more of a dangerous and new-fangled cult.

- **They were secretive**. Romans were suspicious of Christians because of their secret worship gatherings. Outsiders misunderstood what exactly happened in the Eucharist, but in their ignorance they often leveled charges of sexual immorality and even cannibalism against Christians.

These suspicions led to local and regional uprisings against Christians. The two most famous were in Lyons in the year 177, where a popular uprising lynched dozens of Christians by sending them to the arena to die; and in Asia Minor, where a mob lynched the Christian bishop Polycarp (d. 165).

Christian bravery in the face of persecution often won them respect and converts. Even some prominent non-Christian sources, including the philosopher-Emperor Marcus Aurelius, acknowledged the fearlessness with which Christians faced death.

The second century proved critical to Christianity's development, but the next two centuries saw massive changes that changed Christian communities forever.

Chapter 3

Christianity in a Time of Transition

If we knew about the Roman Empire only from TV and movies, we might think of an uninterrupted era of strength and power before a "collapse" in the fifth century. Watching the movie *Gladiator*, for instance, you'd be hard pressed to figure out the empire was suffering through destabilizing Germanic invasions and a debilitating plague, most likely the first manifestation of measles or smallpox. Historians often speak of a "Pax Romana," or Roman peace: the period of general stability from 27 BCE (when Augustus Caesar began to reign, ending a period of civil war) to around 180 CE (after the death of the emperor Marcus Aurelius). Things changed dramatically in the third century, when the Roman Empire nearly disintegrated, beset by internal and external crises.

Rome on the Verge

Between "Barbarian" incursions on the border, a plague under Marcus Aurelius and a severe economic crisis, demographic and social upheaval rocked the empire in the early 200s. To be sure, there had been political instability and civil war before, but it was normally confined to brief periods when ruling dynasties changed hands. The imperial crown, once the possession of a few noble families from largely Roman origin, became the prize for a series of usurpers, warriors, and generals. The period from 235–284 saw twenty-two emperors in forty-nine years, with some reigning for just a few months. Then as now, people sought explanations for why the situation was so much worse.

The same anxiety also explains the changed relationship of Christianity to the state. In 202, the Emperor Septimus Severus launched the first systematic attempt to persecute Christians. That purge took many lives, including two prominent female martyrs, **Perpetua and Felicitas**, killed in North Africa in 202.

Of more far more significance were the persecutions under the Emperor Decius in 251 and Valerian in 258. The Valerian persecution is notable because it was aimed at Christian clergy, by requiring them to produce a *libellus*. A *libellus* was a certificate demonstrating a person had participated in imperial worship, and anyone who refused to obtain one was at best unpatriotic, possibly offending the gods, and at worst subversive. Christians were faced with some tough choices:

- **Flight.** Some Christians fled the persecution and hid out in the countryside or the desert. They defended their actions by citing the general consensus that one should not openly seek martyrdom.

- **Trickery.** Some purchased forged certificates to demonstrate that they had sacrificed, when they had not.

- **Martyrdom.** Many did not flee or buy a *libellus*. When confronted by the authorities, they refused to comply and were arrested, and some were executed publicly.

- **Luck.** The Decian persecution was particularly stringent in Rome and in North Africa, but many Christians managed to avoid persecution altogether because some local authorities simply could not stomach the practice of persecution.

The political situation changed dramatically with the rise of Diocletian in 284. Diocletian completely overhauled the empire, transforming it, in many ways, into a military dictatorship. In the process he might have rescued it from implosion for another several hundred years. Unfortunately, he was responsible for unleashing the most severe persecution of Christians. In 303 he began a local persecution in Nicomedia, his capital city in what is now Turkey, just across the Bosphorus from present-day Istanbul. This persecution lasted almost a decade, in fits and starts, from 303–312, and eventually spread to encompass most of Asia Minor, the Middle East, Egypt, and North Africa. Thousands of Christians were martyred, even more sent to work in the salt mines or to become rowers on ships' slave galleys.

Theological Developments

Along with these persecutions taking their toll on the still-new religion, Christianity also had to deal with several other issues. In particular, a form of Plato's philosophy, called **Neo-Platonism**, emerged and became quite influential. Plato believed in a creative force, one that was hopelessly "other" and differentiated from the created world. He thought the created world was the work of a lesser being, a Second God or Demiurge. The created world was tragically corruptible; everything in this creation was a pale shadow of the perfect models that appeared in the divine sphere. Neo-Platonism grafted onto this philosophy a spiritual quest: the soul, trapped in the body, could free itself from the body and ascend back to The One, or that creative divine force, through meditation, prayer, and contemplation of the divine.

Among Christians, it became quite common to identify Jesus with the "Second God" or Demiurge of the Platonic creation. Not everyone approved of such accommodations. For instance, **Tertullian** (d. 225), a church father writing in the third century and living in North Africa, didn't think Christians should study pagan philosophy—or, for that matter, go to public spectacles in the amphitheaters or anywhere near emperor worship or other unseemly activities. **Origen** (d. 254), the other great theologian of the third century, traveled a different path. He studied philosophy extensively and incorporated Platonic principles and concepts (including his view that the Son was subordinate to the Father).

Yet another of the major theological issues gripping the churches was the question of the power to forgive sins. Some felt baptism should cleanse believers from sin, and that grave sins committed after baptism—such as denying Christ in the midst of persecution—could not be forgiven. Some people postponed baptism until later in life just to make sure that, if they died, they would be sinless (as St. Augustine famously said, "Save me, Lord—but not yet.") Some thought the lapsed needed to be rebaptized before they could be readmitted to the church. Who could make the call? Often the **confessors**, or those who had suffered under persecution and thus earned honor in their communities, were granted the authority to determine the punishment for those who had lapsed. But was their authority equal to that of a bishop? Who really had the authority to forgive sins?

These debates led to a host of schisms and excommunications. **Novatian**, one of the rival bishops of Rome, led a rigorist party and formed a separate church, the Novatians. Meanwhile, **Cyprian** (d. 258) was the bishop of Carthage and one of the leading proponents of readmitting the lapsed back to the church. He called a large synod in North Africa that agreed with his position—and promptly declared those who disagreed with them to be outside of the church. In effect he excommunicated Novatian's followers.

With the rise of more persecutions in 303–313, debates about the nature of the church, the place of baptism, and the readmission of the lapsed all returned full

> Whoever is separated from the Church . . . is separated from the promises of the Church; nor can the one who forsakes the Church of Christ attain to the rewards of Christ. That person is a stranger; profane; an enemy. One can no longer have God for one's Father, if one does not have the church one's mother."
>
> Cyprian of Carthage (d. 258), *On the Unity of the Church.*

Figure 6 The surviving frescoes from the house church in Dura Europos, on the Iraq/Syria border. Note the women approaching the tomb in the lower right hand side.

force. Eventually another rigorist party formed, under the leadership of Donatus, giving name to a breakaway rigorist church in North Africa called the Donatists. Like the Novatians, the Donatists denied the validity of sinful or unworthy clergypeople.

Accounts like these only make up part of Christian life in the ancient world; Christianity also spread to the fringes of the Roman world. Notice the well-preserved Christian house church in Dura Europos on the borderlands of the empire, in Syria near the Iraqi border. There's even some tentative evidence of Christian communities in India.

While shaped by its Roman context, Christianity was never contained by a single culture or context.

Chapter 4

Christianity and Christendom

Sometimes church change takes time. Then there is the case of the turn of the fourth century, when Christianity practically changed overnight.

Constantine: Everything Changes

Constantine's father, Constantius, ruled the western half of the Roman Empire under Diocletian. When Constantius died in 306, his troops declared their loyalty to his son **Constantine**. A predictable series of uprisings, rebellions, and civil wars ensued, and Constantine eventually marched on Italy. In the year 312 he faced an important battle with his rival for emperor in the West.

We do not know exactly what happened next, since sources differ. The best we can gather is that Constantine chose to trust in the God of the Christians to help him in battle. His army seems to have affixed some kind of Christian symbol to their shields. Constantine was victorious in the Battle of the Milvian Bridge in 312, ascribed that victory to the God of the Christians, entered Rome, and was proclaimed emperor in the western portion of the empire. In 313 he met with his counterpart, Licinius, the emperor of the eastern half, and they issued the Edict of Milan. This edict legalized Christianity by allowing for religious tolerance to all religions, including Christians, and marked an end to systemic imperial persecutions. Intrigue and civil war would continue, resulting in 324 with Constantine defeating Licinius and becoming sole ruler of the Roman Empire.

Constantine's policy toward the Christian Church would change Christianity forever. As late as 311 Christians were savagely persecuted in the eastern half of the empire. In 313, toleration was proclaimed, and Constantine began a policy of actively favoring Christianity. Property confiscated in the persecution was returned, and he embarked on an ambitious program of church building. He sent his mother, **Helena**, to Jerusalem, where the Church of the Holy Sepulchre was built over the site of Jesus's tomb. There is some debate about whether he was ever a practicing Christian—he postponed his baptism until his death, which was not unusual at the time—but there can be no doubt that he favored the Christian Church.

Many people see Constantine's favor as the advent of the marriage of "church" and "state." But keep in mind that, for much of the time period we're covering in this book, people would not have understood "church" and "state" as separate, distinct categories. They wouldn't have necessarily thought such separation as wise or prudent, nor would they have thought Constantine was interfering in religious affairs. As emperor, he believed it was his role to help preserve peace and order, an order entrusted to him by divine power. He ascribed his victory to the Christian God, so this was the God to whom he was accountable. Intervening in church disputes was not meddling, but part of his responsibility.

And intervene he did.

The Arian Controversy

Sometime after the Great Persecution, probably around 318, a theological kerfuffle emerged in Alexandria, the second city of the empire. One of the prominent priests of the city, **Arius**, took issue with the language his bishop, Alexander, used to describe the relationship between God the Father and God the Son (Arius couldn't abide placing the Son on par with the Father). Both sides appealed to their colleagues and friends throughout the empire for support. Constantine was forced to call a gathering of bishops in 325 in the city of Nicaea in Asia Minor.

Before getting into the Council of Nicaea, it's important to re-emphasize that Christianity was largely regional and local. With no centralized authority, Christianity developed with particular local emphases, customs, and practices. Creeds had begun to emerge, but no single creed defined the relationship between God the Father and Jesus. Under Constantine, with persecution over and greater communication, these diverse strands now came into contact with one another. One extreme claimed there was just one God, who appeared in three "modes" as Father, Son, and Holy Spirit; the other end ventured toward polytheism, as if the Son and the Holy Spirit were divine entities in their own right. Because of Constantine, they now had a mechanism to adjudicate differences and to enforce decisions.

The Council of Nicaea

Constantine summoned the Council in 325, invited all the bishops in the empire to attend, and paid for their travel and lodging. The result was the largest and most geographically diverse gathering of Christians ever up to that point: about 318 bishops and another 1,500 priests and deacons who came to assist and advise their bishops.

Barely fourteen years removed from systemic persecution, nearly two thousand clergy from all over the empire attended a gathering called and paid for by the emperor. Who said change comes slowly?

The Council drew up a statement of belief, which we now call the **Nicene Creed** (though the form used today dates from

Figure 7 Constantine presiding over the Council of Nicaea, with Arius depicted as the condemned heretic at their feet.

a council in Constantinople in 381). The key word in the statement is the Greek word ***homoousios***: that Jesus was literally "of the same substance" with God the Father. Jesus was not a different being than God the Father. Of course, Arius didn't think Jesus was *not* divine; he just couldn't imagine that Jesus shared the same essence or being as God the Father. Still, by including *homoousios*, the Creed of Nicaea precisely excluded Arius' position.

Nicaea offered solutions to other questions as well. It fixed the date of Easter, rejecting the local practices that still celebrated it in

conjunction with Passover, by introducing the system for calculating Easter that
we use today. It passed a series of "canons," or rules, to be followed by churches
throughout the empire, like having three
bishops present to consecrate a new bishop (a practice that holds today).

With all that painstaking work, Nicaea
didn't exactly settle matters. Far from it.
Instead, the Nicene Creed set off nearly
sixty years of continued conflict, debate,
and discussion about the relationship be-
tween God the Father and God the Son. Another council in 381 reissued the Nicene Creed, with an additional section clarifying the
place and role of the Holy Spirit. A trio of prominent theologians
from the Roman province of Cappadocia (in what is now central
Turkey) provided the theological depth to the Nicene *homoousios*.
The **Cappadocian theologians** included Basil, bishop of the city
of Caesarea; Gregory, his brother, and later bishop of the city of
Nyssa; and their mutual friend Gregory, later bishop of Constantinople. The Cappadocians are credited with drawing a distinc-
tion between "person" and "substance." They argued that God the
Father and Jesus shared a common, divine essence ("substance")
which, in turn, was manifested in differing "persons"—so there
could be a commonality and a sharing.

> "And if you ask about the price of bread, the reply is, 'The Father is greater, and the Son subject to him.' If you say, 'Is the bath ready?,' they declare the Son has his being from the non-existent."
>
> Gregory of Nyssa,
> On the Divinity of the Son
> and the Holy Spirit.

Constantine's Legacy

Constantine's ascent fundamentally reshaped Christianity. The
number of Christians exploded in the fourth century, from maybe
5 to 10 percent of the population, clustered in cities in the Eastern
half, to perhaps half the population of the empire. There was a
massive program of church building. Bishops especially gained
significant influence and authority, as the boundaries of dioceses

were fixed to match with Roman administrative units. Bishops also received legal authority to settle certain disputes once tried in Roman courts.

Eventually, Roman emperors shifted from favoring Christianity to establishing Christianity as the official religion. In the 380s, the emperor **Theodosius** declared Christianity, as defined by the Nicene Creed, as the only legal and legitimate Christian expression. He also outlawed various non-Christian practices, thus formally promoting not just Christianity over other religions, but one version of Christianity over others. With that move we have the advent of Christendom: the fusion or overlapping of church, state, and society that would last over a thousand years in the West.

Some maintain Constantine warped the counter-cultural, first-century Christian vision and made the religion an extension of the state and society. In the Eastern Orthodox Churches, he is considered a saint and given the honorific "Equal to the Apostles" for his work to spread the Christian message. Regardless of how we understand Constantine's legacy, there is one thing we can agree on: Christianity in the year 380 bore little resemblance to the same religion in 310.

Chapter 5

The End of the Beginning:
Early Medieval Christianity

Regarding the battle that marked the turn of the tide in the Second World War, Winston Churchill famously said: "Now this is not the end. It is not even the beginning of the end. But it is, perhaps, the *end of the beginning.*" Four chapters into this book, we are still in the early centuries of Christianity. That should tell you just how formative these early centuries were in the development of Christianity. As we come to the end of the beginning, we can speed the pace a bit to enter the so-called Middle Ages.

The "Fall" of Rome

The Middle Ages are generally divided into three periods: Early (600–1050), High (1050–1300), and Late (1300–1500). The period following the disintegration of the Western Roman Empire (traditionally given as 476) through the reign of Charlemagne (d. 814) is often popularly referred to as the **Dark Ages**. You might think people wandered around hundreds of years, wearing animal skins and ignorant of just about everything, kind of like a Mad Max movie. While there were indeed some challenges in this time period, it was also a formative one for the West.

A major turning point is the so-called **Fall of the Roman Empire**, though we should be wary of the term. Rather than a fall, there was a slow, gradual disintegration of imperial authority, with a steady stream of migrating Teutonic peoples (a much better term than "barbarian," since some of these societies were relatively sophisticated) passing in succession through Europe. Hardly anyone could claim to have true political control over the Western Empire after 400. There arose instead a series of local and regional kingdoms. Then there was Rome itself: a bustling metropolis of close to a million people in the year 1 CE where some people had hot and cold running water, by the year 600 it had shrunk to a shell of itself, with crumbled buildings, defunct aqueducts and maybe forty thousand inhabitants.

The West disintegrated politically. But where the empire diminished, the Church came to take over much of its organizational reach. The Roman system and code of law became the foundation for the West. Even the migrating Teutonic peoples adopted much from the conquered empire around them. Many converted to Christianity and translated the Bible into their own languages, and they all turned to the class of scribes and civil servants who had worked under the Romans to be administrators in their new kingdoms. Far from a "break" and a "fall," what would it mean to name what was happening as the continued transformation and adaptation of the Roman world? And if that is true, what would become of Christianity with the decline of Roman authority?

Monasticism

Before you start to picture huge medieval Gothic monasteries, be aware that monasticism in the period from 400 to 600 is a different creature than its later medieval forms. Monastic communities in the West were generally much smaller, probably no bigger than ten to fifteen monks.

Monasticism arose in the third century and began to flourish in the fourth century. Earlier generations thought you had to be a martyr or suffer under persecution to prove you were a hardcore

Christian. Monasticism was another way, as Christians went to the deserts of Egypt to live lives of prayer, fasting, and self-denial.

Two basic types of monasticism developed: individual (people lived as hermits) and communal (people lived in groups). Both types proliferated in the eastern half of the empire. In the West the communal model predominated. In particular the **Rule of St. Benedict** (480–540), the founder of the abbey of Monte Cassino, became the standard for Western monasticism.

One of the marks of Benedict's rule was its sense of balance. First was the balance between work, prayer, and study. Communities were expected to be self-supporting and self-sustaining, and everyone worked. Prayer was structured for the various times of the day, but it wasn't nearly as elaborate as what emerged later. His rule also proved notable for its vows. In addition to the common vows

Figure 8 Monastic manuscript, twelfth century, depicting St. Benedict giving his Rule to the monks.

of poverty and chastity, he required a vow of stability so monks would remain in the monastery, which improved the sense of continuity, security, and stability in a monastic community. Benedict's rule heavily influenced the subsequent development of Western monasticism.

Celtic Christianity

The missionary work of **St. Patrick** (died around 460) established Christianity in Ireland, planting the seeds for Celtic Christianity to dominate in what is now Ireland, parts of Wales, and northern Scotland. In Britain, with the collapse of Roman rule, a series of invasions followed and much of what is now England reverted to the paganism of the invading Angles, Saxons, Jutes, and others.

Celtic Christianity looked quite different from the parish-diocese model developing throughout Western Europe. Instead,

Figure 9 Remains of monastic huts and monastery graveyard, Skellig Michael, off the west coast of Ireland.

monks and abbots became the most important people in the Celtic Church, at the expense of bishops, who served largely as something like spiritual advisors. Above all, Celtic Christians were known for their missionary work. Columbanus (d. 615) founded monasteries in northern France and throughout the Frankish kingdoms. **Columba** (d. 597) traveled north to the island of Iona off Scotland, where he founded an important monastery whose current incarnation continues to shape Christian life today. Monks from Iona played a prominent role in missionary work in Scotland and what is now northern England. They eventually clashed with the Pope's missionaries, who sought to introduce Roman Christianity as they worked their way up from the south.

The Rise of the Bishop of Rome

Along with monasticism, the episcopacy also took on greater significance. In many areas, bishops become the chief missionaries. There was Martin, bishop of Tours (d. 397), who planted churches in much of what is now southern France. Patrick, mentioned above, took responsibility for bringing Christianity to Ireland, as Ninian (d. 430) did in Britain, Willibrord (d. 739) did in Holland and Belgium, and Boniface (d. 754) did in Germany.

Within this context, it's only natural that the bishop of Rome would become more important. There weren't many bishoprics founded by apostles in the West, and Rome could draw on the authority of not one apostle but the two greatest, Peter and Paul. The bishop exerted no direct power or influence outside of his own see, but others often consulted with him for his opinion. It's worth mentioning that the bishop of Rome's claim to be the successor to Peter was hotly debated; Cyprian, bishop of Carthage in Africa in the third century, claimed all bishops were successors to Peter as the first bishop, not just the bishop of Rome.

In addition to his rising ecclesial power, the bishop of Rome took on increasing authority in central Italy. By the fifth century, a tremendous power vacuum had opened up in Rome. The

Figure 10 Mosaic of Gregory the Great, Worcester College, Oxford. The Holy Spirit, symbolized as a dove, is dictating his writing to him.

city was sacked more than once in the 400s, and the population dwindled. The church stepped up to appoint deacons as administrators over each of the city's seven sections, and the bishop of Rome took over certain civic titles, like Pontifex Maximus, originally a Roman term for the head of the college of pagan priests in Rome and held by the emperor (the Pope still uses the title to this day).

These two factors—the importance of monasticism and the bishop of Rome—merge in the life and work of **Gregory the Great**. A native Roman, Gregory served as bishop of Rome from 590–604. He was one of the first monastics to become Pope, and he gave much of his inheritance to endow monasteries and other charitable organizations sorely in need in the devastated city of Rome. As bishop of Rome, he asserted his authority, particularly when the archbishop of Constantinople began to use the title "Ecumenical" (in Greek meaning the whole world) Patriarch. He sent missionaries to England in 597 to re-Christianize the country. He was also a prolific writer and devoted great energy to revitalizing worship, including introducing a style of plainchant that came to be known as—you guessed it—Gregorian chant.

Troubled Times . . . Again

After centuries of erosion of Roman authority and political instability, Europe finally began to catch its breath by the 600s. The migrating Teutronic peoples eventually settled
down, and northern Europe was divided into
several Germanic kingdoms. The Franks adopted Catholic Christianity under King Clovis
and settled in the area that became what we
call France, and Gothic peoples settled what
is now Spain. Britain remained a network of
small kingdoms, and other Frankish kings and
lower nobility held sway in Germany.

Figure 11
Coronation of
Charlemagne
by Pope Leo.

Nothing marked this shift toward calm
more definitively than the reign of **Charlemagne**, King of the Franks from 768 to 814. On Christmas
Day in the year 800, the Pope crowned Charlemagne emperor in
the West. Charlemagne's coronation as emperor revived a notion
of Christendom as a single Christian world, under one temporal
ruler, the emperor, and one ecclesiastical ruler, the Pope. Charlemagne also enacted numerous reforms in the church, revived
learning, adopted the Rule of Benedict as the standard for monasticism, and forcibly expanded Christianity, famously offering one
of his vanquished foes death or baptism.

All these advances fell apart after Charlemagne, who divided
the empire among his sons in Frankish fashion. Infighting between
his heirs, combined with centuries of Viking raids, disrupted the
brief Carolingian renaissance.

But it didn't turn back the advancing tide of Christianity. The
religion created new structures to respond to the erosion of the
empire in the West, and it changed as it interacted with new cultures like the Germanic peoples and Islam. The transformation
only deepens by the middle of the Medieval period.

Chapter 6

Christianity Goes Medieval

Beginning with the late ninth century, Christianity is very much on the move, growing and expanding, becoming more global and adapting with each new encounter.

Of Emperors, Popes, and Reform

In the tenth century, we get what my church history professor used to refer to as the "Frankenstein's monster Papacy." **Otto** (d. 972) was crowned emperor in the West by the pope, and took quite an interest in reforming the papacy. Successive German emperors intervened regularly in the politics of central Italy, deposing and appointing popes. Seeking to reform the papacy, the German emperors created Frankenstein's monster: an institution that rose up against its reforming masters and changed the relationship between the Church and the empire.

As Charlemagne's empire fell apart, monasticism fell on hard times. Monasteries were coming under the control of the local nobility. To prevent interference from local lords, the **Abbey of Cluny** was founded in 909 and placed directly under the control of the pope. Cluny devoted itself to observing the Rule of

Figure 12 Drawing of the abbey of Cluny, eighteenth century, once the largest in Europe, sacked during the French Revolution and currently in ruins.

St. Benedict, and it so inspired other monasteries that the monks were soon managing a kind of franchise model, with a central abbey directly controlling its daughter communities. Unfortunately, as Cluny acquired wealth and land, it strayed from the reforming path. A group of monks founded a new abbey in Citeaux, striving once again for a strict observance of the Rule of Benedict. They birthed the **Cistercian Order**, which peaked under the charismatic abbot Bernard of Clairvaux (d. 1153).

Soon these reforming streams came together, as the German emperors, interested in reforming the papacy and liberating it from the squabbles of local Roman politics, turned to the monastic reform movement to recruit new popes. They found two of them in **Leo IX** (d. 1054) and **Gregory VII** (d. 1085). Both enforced clerical celibacy to prevent clergy from passing down their churches to their children. They also reformed the "gifts" clergy gave in "thanksgiving" for their appointment to church offices, which smacked of paying to be appointed—the sin of simony.

What they could not manage was a recalibration of the relationship between the Church and lay authority. Nobody doubted that the monarch and the pope were both divinely chosen by God to rule; the argument was over the influence of lay versus clerical authority in appointing bishops. The struggle between popes and emperors continued until a compromise was struck, whereby the Church invested bishops with symbols of ecclesiastical office and the emperor or lay ruler passed along the other symbols of authority.

Monastic reform kept moving forward, apart from (and sometimes in response against) the state powers. **Francis of Assisi** (d. 1226) was determined to return to the "basics" of Christianity, eschewing the wealth that had become common among medieval monks. The Franciscans wore simple gray tunics and begged for their sustenance. **Dominic of Caleruega,** Spain (d. 1221) founded the Dominican Order. These monks were devoted to learning and preaching, as their official name indicated—"The Order of Preachers"—and they often used those gifts to preach against heresies that sprang up during the Middle Ages.

The two orders produced some of the Church's foremost theologians, luminaries like St. Bonaventure and St. Thomas Aquinas. Monks also served as missionaries to China and eventually Africa and the "New" World of North America. On the downside, they also served as some of the most zealous inquisitors rooting out heresy, especially during the Crusades.

The Crusading Movement

Christian detractors today are quick to point to the Crusades as proof of Christian colonialism and cruelty. How did this difficult chapter begin? Within a hundred years of Muhammad's death in 632, Islam had burst out of the Arabian peninsula and spread across the Holy Land, Asia Minor, Egypt, North Africa, and into Spain, as well as what is now Iran and Iraq. The Frankish kings managed to turn back Muslim advances into what is now France, and successive sieges of Constantinople were repelled.

In 1095 **Pope Urban** called for a Crusade to recapture the Holy Land. The "First" Crusade (1096–1099) captured Jerusalem and the holy places, but the Muslim world regrouped, recaptured Jerusalem, and threatened and eventually retook the European outposts in the Holy Land. In the end, the Crusading movement fizzled out, but not without taking a toll on Christianity's relations with its neighbors for centuries to come.

It is hard to look at the Crusades without seeing them through a post-9/11 lens. Crusaders made little attempt to understand Muslim culture and simply transplanted Western European feudal society to the Holy Land. The Crusading movement also made the schism between Eastern and Western Christianity permanent; Greek Christians harbored bitter enmity toward the Crusaders for capturing and sacking Constantinople in 1204.

From 1100 to 1400, Christians unleashed violent persecutions against Jews. There were also sustained efforts to define and exterminate "heresy," including crusades against those deemed heretics

Figure 13 In one of the lowest points of the Crusades, Christians sacked Constantinople in 1204 instead of going to the Holy Land.

within the Christian fold. The famous line, "Kill them all, God will know his own," is ascribed to Arnaud Amalric (d. 1225), the Cistercian abbot the pope appointed to head the Albigensian Crusade against heretics in southern France.

New Developments in Theology: Scholasticism

Far from the battlefields, **the Scholastics** (so-called because they owed allegiance to different "schools" of thought) were advancing the life of the mind. **Anselm** (d. 1109), archbishop of Canterbury and one of the first scholastic theologians, believed people could use reason to better understand the Christian faith. His classic work *Why God Became Man* outlined his theology of the atonement (how Jesus reconciled humanity to God): Through Adam's sin, which we all inherit, humanity owed a debt to God. God could not simply forgive the sin—the debt had to be repaid. So God became human and died to pay it.

The greatest of the scholastic theologians was undoubtedly **St. Thomas Aquinas** (d. 1274). Aquinas was a Dominican monk and graduate of the University of Paris, and he published a massive theological commentary called the *Summa Theologica*. In it he applied the philosophy of Aristotle to construct five proofs for the existence of God. Scholastics like Aquinas had their share of detractors, as many thought their work highly speculative. This led to the oft-ascribed charge that they would argue over "how many angels could dance on the head of a pin."

The Fourteenth Century: Plague and Schism

A devastating plague tore through western Europe in the 1340s, claiming the lives of up to a third of the population and opening up deep rifts between rich and poor, Jewish and Christian. Meanwhile, the papacy moved from Rome to Avignon, in what is now France, where it developed the system we know as the modern papal "**curia**": the sophisticated bureaucracy responsible for governing and organizing the church and collecting taxes and revenues.

In 1378 Pope Gregory IX returned to Rome (convinced, in part, by the Dominican **Catherine of Siena**, one of the more remarkable women of the Middle Ages) . . . only to die shortly thereafter. The cardinals met and elected an Italian bishop as pope; however, a smaller group of cardinals claimed they were unduly influenced by the Roman crowds, so they met and elected a rival pope based in Avignon.

And now we come to what historians call the **Great Western Schism**, when two rival popes ruled the Church from 1378 to 1417, each having so much support they split Europe almost evenly. People realized the schism was a scandal, but nobody knew how to end it, since neither pope would back down. Eventually a group of cardinals took matters in their own hands and elected a third pope, hoping the other two would resign. They didn't, so for a couple more years there were three popes.

Eventually the crisis swelled so far the Church's leaders had to revive an old idea: call a church council. Gathered in the city of Constance (in what is now Switzerland), the council settled the schism. One pope resigned, and the council took an extraordinary step and deposed the other rival pope. A new pope, Martin V, was elected in 1417 and secured the allegiance of almost all the rulers in Europe. Within a few decades, the papacy was stronger than ever.

The Humanist Renaissance

The humanist movement began in the late fourteenth century and stretched to the early sixteenth century, making it an important precursor to the Reformation. Why was it called humanism? Simply put, because it focused on humankind rather than on God, elevating poetry, philosophy and art alongside theology. It was the time of Dante and Petrarch and the beginnings of artistic revivals in Italy and beyond. More importantly for our purposes, there was an increased emphasis on scholarship and learning.

Refugees from Constantinople, conquered by the Turks in 1453, brought along a treasure trove of ancient manuscripts Western Europe had never seen. Scholars were excited to learn Greek and Hebrew so they could access these treasures. The greatest exponent of the humanist movement was **Desiderius Erasmus** (d. 1536). Erasmus was the foremost scholar of his generation, and he crafted a scholarly edition of the Greek New Testament, published in 1516. Up to this point, Western Christians used the **Latin Vulgate** version of the scriptures, the standard since the 400s. With access to ancient Greek manuscripts, Erasmus was determined to introduce a more accurate translation. In the process, he undermined aspects of the medieval church's authority.

Consider this example: In Matthew 3, the Latin Vulgate translates John the Baptist's speech to the crowds as "Do penance, for the kingdom of heaven is at hand." That verse had everything to do with the development of the sacrament of confession in the medieval church. Erasmus noticed the Greek verb was *metanoia*, which literally means to "change one's mind," in the sense of changing one's ways or amending one's life. That's not quite what the medieval church meant by the sacrament of penance. Erasmus stuck to his research and said the phrase could be understood as "Repent, the kingdom of heaven is at hand."

Humanist scholarship had the potential to spark trouble. For, while diversity had marked Christianity for its whole life, some differences couldn't coexist peacefully.

Chapter 7

Reformations Without End

In September of 1561, a group of Christians in the French city of Poissy, inspired by the theology of John Calvin, entered a gathering clad in distinctive, long, black gowns. Audible hisses could be heard from gathered Roman Catholic bishops. The gathering had been called by the monarchy to try to mediate between different religious factions, but reconciliation failed and eventually France descended into civil war.

The sixteenth century was a century of dramatic upheavals. Far from a single Reformation, scholars now speak of the "Reformations" or "Reformation Era." By the year 1600, European culture and religious life looked profoundly different than it did in 1500.

Political, Social, and Cultural Change

The Reformation period could not have happened without some key political, cultural, social, religious, and technological developments in the fifteenth and sixteenth centuries.

- **Politics**: For the first time, we can begin to speak about France, England, and Spain as nation-states with shared identities, where earlier they were more or less hodgepodges of different languages, cultures, and political systems. Even in places that remained politically fragmented, like Germany, the rise of vernacular languages helped to create a sense of shared cultural identity.

- **Economics**: As cities began to recover from the shocks of the fourteenth century, people returned to urban life. This led, in part, to the rise of a new middle class and disrupted the economic, political, and social expectation of lords (who derived their wealth from land) and serfs (who were bound to that land). It is precisely in some of these towns and cities that reforming ideas took hold.

- **Technology**: Among the many technological advances, none shines brighter than the printing press. Previously, books were time-consuming to make, costly to purchase, and largely produced by the Church. The printing press democratized information in a way perhaps only rivaled by the Internet. Books were now cheaper, quicker to produce, and less susceptible to central control.

  For proof of the power of the printing press, contrast the example of Jan Hus and Martin Luther. Hus was burned at the stake in 1415 and copies of his treatises hunted down and destroyed. Luther's ideas were written in vernacular German and spread quickly as a result of the printing press. Even had he been captured and executed, Luther's message could not have been controlled as Hus's was a century earlier.

Fueled by these political and cultural developments, reform-minded people formed partnerships with various power structures. In areas ruled by counts and dukes, like politically fragmented Germany, these leaders determined whether reformation ideas spread . . . or not. In places ruled by city councils, such as parts of Switzerland and Germany, reformers had to win over elected officials and convince them to adopt reforming ideas. In nation-states (primarily France, Spain, Scandinavia, and England) the monarch had enormous influence in religious matters.

Back to Grace

The Reformations weren't just about politics and printing presses, however. They centered on a message: How could a person access the grace of God?

The medieval Catholic Church developed a sacramental system focused on the ways God's grace is communicated in the **sacraments**, especially the Eucharist. Via the sacraments of baptism, confession, confirmation, the Eucharist, marriage, ordination, and last rites, you could essentially participate in a ritual act and ensure God's grace. Why is this so important? Suppose you perform a Eucharist where no one participates; the grace of Christ's body made present could be counted toward another intention. Likewise, if you went to confession and received absolution, you could substitute something instead of the penance assigned. (This, by the way, is the classical definition of an **indulgence**: it is not paying to have one's sins forgiven, but the substitution of something in place of the penance assigned, or the remission of the penance itself.)

The doctrine of **purgatory** made the whole system work. Purgatory was an intermediate place between heaven and hell, where the burden of one's sins could be alleviated—literally, "purged." The grace communicated in a celebration of the Eucharist on earth could be directed toward alleviating the debt of someone in purgatory. This may sound strange to our modern ears, but keep in mind that death ran rampant in these days. Your mother passed away at a relatively young age? Now you could ease her suffering by paying for a Mass to be said. The wealthy did it regularly: Henry VII of England left enough money for Masses to be said for his soul for perhaps 10,000 years. Middle-class and poor people also invested in the system, but almost all the reformers rebelled against it.

Luther and Lutheranism

Martin Luther (1483–1546) was the son of the new middle classes of the late medieval period. He grew up in one of the growing German towns and attended one of the newly founded universities. All those privileges notwithstanding, Luther was obsessed with doubt: he continually felt he could not be what God wanted him to be. His crisis of faith led him to craft a devastating critique of the excesses of the medieval Catholic Church's understanding of God's grace. Put simply, he said, grace is not something we can earn; it's something we already have and must strive daily to live into.

Luther might have been driven by personal reasons, but he was happy to use politics to get results. He titled one of his tracts "An Appeal to the German People," and by the 1520s some local German rulers and independent German city-states adopted aspects of Luther's ideas. Churches in these areas allowed clergy to marry and offered the Bible and liturgy in German. If no one could do anything to "earn" grace, things like monastic vows and Masses said for the dead made no sense. Monastic money and lands were confiscated, and the Bible took center stage in the Lutheran Reformation, with the rallying cry of *Sola Scriptura*, or "Scripture alone."

A series of armed conflicts—as well as a massive peasant uprising—broke out between the pope's supporters and those who backed Luther. Reform-minded leaders drew up a summary of their ideas to mediate some solution. At one of these gatherings called by the Emperor to mediate, the reformers earned their name, "**Protestants**," because they protested the meeting's condemnation of their ideas. The document Luther and his colleagues drew up, called the Augsburg Confession, became the centerpiece of the Lutheran Reformation and remains a touchstone of Lutheran theology to the present day.

In 1555, after years of conflict between Catholics and Protestants, a truce was brokered in the Holy Roman Empire, the area now encompassing Germany and Austria, called the **Peace of**

Figure 14 Luther defending his beliefs before Charles V at the Diet of Worms, where he supposedly said, "Here I stand. I can do no other."

Augsburg. It permitted localities—whether cities governed by a council or territories ruled by a prince or Lord—to choose which path they would follow, Lutheran or Catholic. This, however, was the ruling authority's decision, not those of individuals: if you happened to be Catholic but your duke chose to be Lutheran, too bad. As a result of the Peace of Augsburg, much of what is now northern Germany became Lutheran, while parts of what is now southern Germany and Austria remained Catholic.

The Reformed Tradition

Meanwhile, other reform movements were developing in what is now France and Switzerland. A prominent leader in the Swiss Reformation was **Ulrich Zwingli** (d. 1531). Like Luther, he took the Bible as an important authority in reforming the church. Unlike Luther, he developed a different understanding of the presence of Christ in the Eucharist. He said Christ was not physically "in" the elements of bread and wine, but present through the collective memorial act of the people. In other words, when Jesus said,

"This is my body. Whenever you eat it, do this in remembrance of me," he was promoting the act of remembering. This core disagreement kept the Swiss reform movement from linking with its German counterpart.

John Calvin (d. 1564) had enormous influence on reform movements in Switzerland, France, England, and Scotland. On the nature of the Eucharist, he staked out a middle ground between Luther and Zwingli. Most people recall his emphasis on "predestination," also present in Paul's letter to the Romans and in St. Augustine's theology. Calvin was certain God had foreordained (or predestined) some to be of the "elect," before they were even born.

Drawing on the New Testament, Calvin envisioned a church governed by elders who were not ordained like clergy. He also placed a greater emphasis on preaching the Word and revived the order of deacon (albeit on a congregational level), doing away with the office of bishops as understood in the medieval church. Calvin's system cast a long shadow, with one strain of churches calling themselves "Presbyterian" (from the word presbyter, for elder), and others calling themselves "Reformed."

In France, those influenced by Calvin's theology and ideas of church governance were called **Huguenots** (whose story we considered at the opening of this chapter). The Reformation in France was a particularly brutal and bloody affair. Protestant ideas spread quickly and rapidly, eventually resulting in a series of civil wars. In August of 1572, Catholic forces organized the St. Bartholomew's Day massacre, when thousands of Protestants were murdered.

Radical Reformation

Still more groups proliferated during the Reformations period, often lumped together under the title of the "radical" Reformation (though many of their ideas wouldn't seem exactly radical now). Take the **Anabaptists**. They insisted you had to make a profession of faith before your baptism, which meant infant baptisms

Maria van Monjou. 1552.

Figure 15 Anabaptists were persecuted by Catholic and Protestants alike. The punishment in some places for rebaptism was execution by drowning.

were invalid. So they baptized one another and earned the title "Anabaptists," or "re-baptizers." Anabaptist groups further antagonized the state by refusing to swear oaths in public. Recall that, in a pre-written society, oral contracts were the glue that held society together. It wasn't unusual for other Christians, both Catholic and reforming, to persecute Anabaptists. The Church of England included a condemnation of Anabaptists in its official theological statement, the Thirty-Nine Articles. In a bizarre twist, Anabaptists were often punished with drowning.

Though radical for their time, Anabaptist ideas flourished and live today among such groups as the Baptists, Mennonites, Amish, and the Church of the Brethren.

The Catholic Response

The Catholic Reformation was once dubbed the "Counter Reformation," usually by Protestant historians who saw it solely as a reaction to reforming ideas. However, plenty of people in Europe in the late 1400s and early 1500s knew the church was in dire need of reform. In fact, several movements for reform predated Luther, most notably in Spain. Lax monastic orders were reformed, and new universities promoted education and learning. New religious orders arose, the most important of which was the **Jesuits**, founded by Ignatius of Loyola. They placed themselves under the control and protection of the pope, wore no distinctive habit, founded schools and pursued mission work overseas, and rapidly grew powerful, wealthy, and influential.

Despite these efforts at reform, the Catholic Church was by and large overwhelmingly hostile to Luther's critique. An Index of Forbidden Books was drawn up, the Inquisition was reestablished under the Papacy's direction (not to be confused with the notorious Spanish Inquisition, which operated directly under royal control in Spain). Eventually, a church council was called in the city of Trent, where it met on and off from 1546 to 1563. The **Council of Trent** gave no middle ground to Luther or Protestant ideas. It specifically condemned Luther's theology of grace and placed the tradition of the Church on equal footing with Scripture, effectively blocking its ears to Protestant critique.

Part II

Chapter 8

This Thing Called Anglicanism

One of the greatest myths about the English Reformation is that it was the result of Henry VIII wanting a divorce. For one thing, technically Henry did not want a divorce: he wanted an annulment of his previous marriage which, in turn, had only been possible because of a special papal dispensation. For another, reducing the Reformation to one person's marital status fails to account for the layers of issues involved. In this chapter, we go much deeper into the story of Reformation in England, a process that lasted more than 200 years.

The Reformation under Henry VIII

Here is the real story: Henry VIII had married his dead brother's widow. Since marrying one's brother's widow was against church law, he needed permission from the pope, which he applied for and received, and the two married. Henry was a staunch religious conservative and wrote a text called *Assertion of the Seven Sacraments* in response to Martin Luther's claims on the Continent. In gratitude, the pope awarded him the title "Defender of the Faith," a title English monarchs still claim at their coronation.

Though Henry's beliefs were traditional, influences from the Lutheran Reformation in Germany began to seep into England. Henry and his chancellor, Cardinal Thomas Wolsey, strongly resisted these influences. **William Tyndale**, who translated the New Testament into English, fell victim to Henry's conservative policy and was executed for his efforts in 1536.

Matters began to change concurrent with Henry's marital problems. Henry wondered if he had been cursed for marrying his brother's widow, and he explored the possibility of getting an annulment of his marriage from Catherine. Henry's chances were slim, thanks to political realities: Catherine's nephew was Charles V, the most powerful man in Europe. There was little chance the pope would reverse a decision by a predecessor *and* offend Charles V.

Henry chose a different tack: to bring the English church under his direct control. He did this with a series of Acts of Parliament that culminated in the **Act of Supremacy in 1534**, which declared the king the head of the Church in England. Yet in some ways this wasn't so different from other parts of Europe, like Spain, where monarchs gained significant control over the Church in their realms.

By the time **Thomas Cranmer** was appointed archbishop of Canterbury in 1533, he was the highest ecclesiastical authority in the realm. Given that appeals to Rome were now forbidden, he granted Henry an annulment.

The Church under Henry

Henry sought to establish a non-papal, traditional Catholic Church within England. Theologically very little had changed by his death in 1547: the Mass was still in Latin, personal confession was the norm, belief in purgatory and clerical celibacy were reaffirmed. The only major liturgical change was placing an English Bible in each church, with a chapter to be read each week (not a small matter, but nowhere near the scope of changes elsewhere in Europe). If there was a major shake-up, it was the dissolution of the English monasteries; their land was confiscated and sold or granted to the nobility. As for political fallout, Sir Thomas More, the king's Chancellor, and Bishop John Fisher of Rochester—two prominent conservatives who refused the royal Supremacy—were executed.

Figure 16 Front page of the first official English Bible, 1539. Henry VIII (with God above his head) handing the Bible to Archbishop of Canterbury Thomas Cranmer on the left and Thomas Cromwell on the right.

The Reformation under Edward

Change, which had been slow under Henry, was rapid under his successor, **Edward VI**. Though crowned in 1547 at age 9, Edward never got the chance to reign in his own right as king (he died in 1553, at age 15). Instead, a Council of Regents ruled in his stead, which included links to prominent reformers. Those leaders pushed changes during Edward's short reign, with Archbishop Thomas Cranmer freed to serve as chief architect.

The first **Book of Common Prayer** was issued in 1549, barely two years into Edward's reign; a second version came out in 1552. The prayer book of 1549 attempted to accomplish several goals, as Thomas Cranmer explained in its preface. One was to have the liturgy in the language of the people, so it could be understood. Another was to simplify matters, so that priests only needed a Bible and the Book of Common Prayer to conduct the liturgy.

The 1552 edition took on a more "Protestant" tone. For instance, it forbade kneeling when people received Communion, and the words spoken when Communion was distributed—"take and eat this in remembrance that Christ died for you"—sounded more like Zwingli's memorialist understanding of the Eucharist.

Reformers instituted a dramatic move known as the "stripping of the altars": statues and images were confiscated, church vessels melted down, and an entire system of popular piety was destroyed. Conservative bishops who resisted the changes were deposed from their sees and prominent reformers elevated. Cranmer also tried to link the changes in England to movements on the Continent, and prominent reformers from Europe were welcomed to England, including Martin Bucer and John Knox.

The Reformation under Mary

The situation took another turn with the death of Edward VI, who had always been sickly, in 1553. **Queen Mary**, Henry's daughter by Catherine of Aragon, sought to return the country to papal obedience. She made two fatal mistakes in this regard. She married her cousin, Philip of Spain, which aroused the hostility of those who feared Spanish domination. She also vigorously persecuted those who had supported reform under Edward. In the five years of her reign, roughly 300 people were executed for religious reasons, earning her the nickname "Bloody Mary." Mary's reign ended with her death in 1558, having provided no heir. The stage was set for Henry's second daughter, Elizabeth, to become queen.

The Elizabethan Settlement

Queen Elizabeth came to the throne in 1558 under unusual circumstances. She was the daughter of Anne Boleyn, Henry's second wife, who was executed in the Tower of London in 1536 largely for the crime of not producing a son. Elizabeth's early life was often surrounded by court intrigue. She was lucky to be alive, since many of Mary's counselors thought the queen should have executed Elizabeth as a rival for the throne. After the tumultuous preceding decade, she needed to find a way to hold England together. Could she honor the desire for continued church reform while satisfying those who thought the situation had gotten out of control under Edward VI's reign?

The results of the Parliament of 1559 are often called the **Elizabethan "Settlement,"** which I am fond of putting in quotation

Figure 17 Elizabeth I presiding over Parliament, which would try to find a lasting religious compromise for England.

marks, since one could reasonably argue it didn't "settle" anything definitively. There were several aspects to the Settlement:

- The Royal Supremacy was reintroduced, with the monarch now called Supreme Governor, instead of Supreme Head, of the Church.

- The Book of Common Prayer was reissued, with several efforts to find theological common ground. For instance, the words at the administration of the bread and wine were a mash-up of the 1549 and 1552 books. In the 1549 version, the priest gave communicants the bread with the words, "The body of our Lord Jesus Christ, given for you, preserve your body and soul unto everlasting life." In the 1552 book, the priest said simply, "Take and eat this, in remembrance that Christ died for thee, and feed on him in thy heart by faith, with thanksgiving." The 1559 book combined both: "The body of our Lord Jesus Christ, given for you, preserve your body and soul unto everlasting life; take and eat this, in remembrance that Christ died for thee, and feed on him in thy heart by faith, with thanksgiving."

- As with Henry, these parliamentary acts also came with enforcement. Those who absented themselves from worship in the Church of England were subject to monetary fines.

While it is likely Henry, and later Elizabeth, held out hope for some kind of reconciliation with the papacy, matters changed in 1570 when the pope excommunicated Elizabeth and released her subjects from any oaths of loyalty to her. This was not just a religious act: The Pope was, in essence, calling on the English people to overthrow their monarch. Anti-Catholic tendencies hardened in 1588, when Catholic Spain attempted to invade England with the Spanish Armada. Practicing Roman Catholicism was thus considered tantamount to treason and un-English, inaugurating a nasty anti-Catholic streak to Anglican-Roman Catholic relations that would last centuries.

Anglicanism Takes Shape

During Elizabeth's reign, we see efforts to flesh out an understanding of what the Church of England actually *was*. **John Jewel** responded directly to arguments from the Roman Catholic Church in his work *Apology for English Christianity*. He also developed the idea that the Church of England was the restoration of a purer, apostolic form of English Christianity after centuries of accretion and corruption of the Western Catholic Church. English leaders issued a theological statement, the **Thirty-Nine Articles**, which made it clear that the Church of England continued in the historic Christian faith and struck a balance between Lutheran and Reformed understandings.

In the latter years of Elizabeth's reign, **Richard Hooker** (d. 1603) introduced some of the most distinctive aspects of Anglican theology. Hooker was responding, in part, to charges leveled both from Roman Catholics and from those who argued for continued reform in the Church of England. Hooker stepped forward to chart a middle path between the conflicted sides, to defend the Church of England, the Prayer Book, episcopacy, and an Anglican understanding of the sacraments against both the Puritans who wanted to continue the reformation and the Catholics who thought the Church of England was no church at all.

In a manifesto titled *Of the Laws of Ecclesiastical Polity*, Hooker addressed a host of issues:

- **Authority**: Roman Catholics argued that authority came from the papacy. Meanwhile, reformers said the Bible should be the only authority. In response, Hooker explained authority had to be balanced between three sources: Scripture, Tradition, and Reason. Anglicans love to refer to this as a **"three-legged stool,"** though Hooker never used the analogy.

- **Participation**: The most original element Hooker developed is that of participation with the incarnate Christ, an important aspect of Anglican sacramental understanding. For Hooker the grace of the sacraments lies not only in the elements of the sacraments, but in the way they can transform the receiver. He believed we would receive a "mystical transubstantiation in us, a true change of soul and body."

• **English identity**: He also wove religious, cultural, and national identity together. To be English, he argued, was to be a member of the Church of England, and to be a member of the Church of England was to be English.

Just When You Thought It Was Over . . .

If you thought the English Reformation itself was a violent and turbulent affair, the situation became worse in the seventeenth century. Elizabeth's death in 1603 without an heir (she never married) resulted in the accession of **James Stuart**, king of Scotland, the son of Elizabeth's first cousin, Mary, Queen of Scots, who, incidentally, Elizabeth had executed. James was an advocate of what was called the "divine right" theory of kingship: the king was appointed by God, and as such had complete authority. On the religious front, since he was from Presbyterian Scotland, reformers hoped to find an ally in the new king. Those groups included:

• **The Puritans**: So-called because they sought to "purify" the Church of England, these reformers sought further revision of the prayer book. They wanted more Scripture reading and to abolish rites and ceremonies they considered unbiblical: sealing with the sign of the Cross in baptism, and the use of wedding rings in the wedding ceremony, to name a few. Some called for a Presbyterian form of governance of the Church of England.

• **Separatists**: Other groups rejected the notion of a state church in favor of local, gathered communities. These groups were variously called "Separatists," "Anabaptists," or "Independents." One strand of Independents migrated to Holland and later the American colonies, establishing a settlement in Plymouth, Massachusetts. Americans know them as "Pilgrims."

These groups presented James with a list of requests for reform as he journeyed from Scotland to England for his enthronement. In response James called a conference that met in 1604. To their surprise, he uttered the famous line, "No bishop, no king," revealing that he considered the episcopate also divinely instituted, like the monarchy. He rejected nearly all the Puritan demands, though he did commission a new translation of the Bible, issued in 1611, which came to be known as the King James Version.

James became more autocratic, eventually refusing to call Parliament into session and raising money by increasing taxes and levies. His son, Charles I, also refused to call Parliament and polarized religious sentiment in England. Charles appointed **William Laud** as archbishop of Canterbury in 1633, and Laud took a firm line against the Puritans. Authors of certain tracts sometimes had "SL" branded on their cheek, short for "Seditious Libeler." Puritans instead called the SL brand the "Sign of Laud."

Matters came to a head when Laud and Charles attempted to introduce bishops and a prayer book in Scotland in 1637. War broke out when the Scots refused, and Charles had to call Parliament into session to raise the taxes he needed. The situation escalated out of control, and civil war broke out. Eventually Laud was executed.

Civil War and Beyond

The Civil War lasted roughly from 1642 to 1645. **Oliver Cromwell** rose as something like a savior for the Puritans (he apparently thought of himself as the "Puritan Moses"). Cromwell raised an organized, well-trained fighting force called the New Model Army, and they eventually defeated the king, who escaped and attempted to raise a new army. Sure there would be no peace with Charles still alive, the king was beheaded on January 30, 1649.

Figure 18 Execution of Charles I, 1649.
Anglicanism would go underground during
Oliver Cromwell's rule.

Under Cromwell, the prayer book and episcopacy were outlawed, religious toleration was permitted, and Cromwell ruled England essentially as military dictator. Loyal Anglicans mostly lay low.

When Cromwell died in 1658, the people and Parliament were
weary of military dictatorship and brought back the monarchy.
Charles I's son, Charles II, became king in 1660. The question of
religious policy immediately surfaced, and a major conference was
called in 1661. The advocates of episcopacy and the prayer book
were in no mood to compromise. Presbyterianism had come to mean
anarchy, treason, and oppression in their eyes. The prayer book, with
subtle changes, was reissued and conformity was required. Further-
more, another series of legal acts were passed, the so-called **Claren-
don Code**, greatly restricting the rights of non-Anglicans to worship.

The Nonjuring Schism and Toleration

In the latter years of Charles II's reign, the tide turned yet again.
He did not have a male heir, and his brother, James II, was a pro-
fessed Catholic. In 1685 James II became king and began easing

the restrictions against Roman Catholics. In response, Parliament invited Charles II's daughter, an Anglican, who married William, Duke of Orange, from the staunchly Protestant Holland, to England. William raised an army and landed in England. James II fled, and, in what is called the **Glorious Revolution**, William and Mary became joint monarchs.

Under William and Mary, Parliament closed the James II loophole and required that all future monarchs be members of the Church of England, and added that they could marry only members of the Church of England. This law was only recently repealed, which explains (in part) why Kate Middleton had to be confirmed in the Church of England before her royal wedding to Prince William. A Bill of Rights was passed, and, while the monarch kept some limited authority, in effect England officially became a constitutional monarchy. Meanwhile, limited religious toleration was provided for what came to be known as "dissenters." Toleration was still excluded for Unitarians and Roman Catholics, and restrictions were placed on dissenters (for instance, their marriages were not considered legally binding).

But the way was far from smooth. Some held that James II never officially abdicated the throne, and many clergy felt bound to him via the oaths of loyalty taken at ordination in the Church of England. These four hundred parish priests and six bishops, including the archbishop of Canterbury, were eventually ousted from their posts in the Church. Yet another dispute ensued, called the **Nonjuring Schism**, for those who would not swear oaths of loyalty to William and Mary. Several found refuge in Scotland, which was still officially Presbyterian. The episcopal orders of Samuel Seabury, the first American bishop, who was consecrated by Scottish bishops, stem in part from this nonjuring line.

The English Reformation was not a singular, clean, straightforward event. One could argue that it did not "end" until 1688, when Parliament made room for more than one Church in the realm. One could argue that it has never ended, as the Church continues to form and reform to this day.

Chapter 9

Anglicanism Comes to America

As we start exploring Anglicanism in the American colonies, and the very existence of the Episcopal Church, keep in mind one important truth: Anglicanism wasn't meant to be exported.

This may sound odd, considering that today's Anglican Communion is a diverse, widely spread, global church. Yet, for the bulk of two centuries, the Church of England understood itself as a particular expression of Christianity confined to a particular people and a particular geographic location, with a particular relationship between the church and the state.

In 1607, the first permanent English colony in North America was established in Jamestown. In order to get a charter, the Virginia Company had to bring a chaplain from the Church of England and to declare Anglicanism the official church. As England expanded overseas with its colonies, so did the Church of England, but the ecclesiastical expansion was haphazard and full of trial and error. What would this particular expression of Christianity look like when transplanted from its original setting? No one knew for sure.

Religion in the Colonies

Religious expression in colonial America looked different in all the original thirteen colonies, partly because of differences in the colonies themselves.

Some colonies were a lot like Silicon Valley: a new frontier for investment, business, trade, and almost anything else. Many settlements started as money-making operations, and the original ones were trading companies with a clear task: to turn a profit for their investors. Virginia started this way with Jamestown.

Just as special interests define politics today, they controlled royal charters for land in the "New World." Religious groups got their share: the Separatists started the Plymouth colony, and the Puritans launched the Massachusetts Bay colony, creating something akin to a fusion of church and state, where you had to be a church member to vote. Nobles received their piece of the pie: Pennsylvania was a grant to William Penn, and Maryland was given to Lord Baltimore. Each brought his religious proclivities to bear. Penn was a Quaker, so Quakers had a strong presence and allowed religious toleration in the colony. Lord Baltimore, a Roman Catholic, allowed religious toleration to provide a haven for Catholics in Maryland.

England acquired other colonies through conquest and assimilation. New York began as a Dutch colony, and Canada was French, but once conquered, these lands came directly under the Crown. Southern Delaware's assimilation was less violent; its Swedish settlements were absorbed so peacefully, one of the oldest Episcopal Churches in Delaware is called Old Swedes Church.

"Anglicanisms"

Just like we had Judaisms in the time of Jesus, in the colonial period we can speak of Anglicanisms: various forms that developed from region to region.

New England

Except for Rhode Island, in New England the Congregational Church was established by law. These colonies were founded by people who were persecuted by the state church in England, so they viewed Anglicanism with suspicion. Rhode Island was always notable for its religious diversity, including some early Jewish religious communities and the first Baptist church in the colonies. King's Chapel was the first Anglican Church in Boston in 1686 (and, interestingly enough, later one of the most notable Unitarian churches in America).

Mid-Atlantic States

Anglicanism in New York benefited from its relation to the crown. Trinity Episcopal Church on Wall Street in New York City was granted land in lower Manhattan, much of which it never sold; to

Figure 19 Old Swedes Episcopal Church, Wilmington, Delaware. Photo circa 1934.

this day, it is one of the richest parishes in the world. Pennsylvania was founded by Quaker William Penn, but Anglicanism was strong in cosmopolitan Philadelphia, the most important city in the colonial period. Though only 2 percent of Pennsylvania was Anglican by the Revolution, they included some of the most influential people in the colonies.

The South

With the formation of the Virginia House of Burgesses, the state government took over the establishment role Parliament held in England. When new towns were laid out, land was provided for an Anglican church, to be supported by taxation. A similar situation eventually prevailed in Maryland, where the colony reverted to royal hands after Lord Baltimore's death and Anglicanism was established by state law. Anglicanism was also the established church in North Carolina, South Carolina, and Georgia.

Distinctiveness

Even with this regional diversity, at least four distinct elements marked pre-Revolutionary Anglicanism.

The Adaptation of the Vestry System

Originally conceived in England as the means for laypeople to manage church property and social programs, vestries accumulated considerably more power in the colonial period. In Virginia they held the right to choose and appoint clergy. Before long, the other colonies placed vestries in charge of calling a rector and maintaining parish property.

The Development of Missionary Societies

The **Society for the Promotion of Christian Knowledge (SPCK)** provided Bibles, pamphlets, and books for colonial schools, parishes, and libraries. More importantly, the **Society**

for the Propagation of the Gospel in Foreign Parts (SPG) provided people: it paid the salaries for missionaries. SPG missionaries spread the gospel to Native Americans and slaves, and contributed to the significant spread of Anglicanism to previously Congregational New England. Without these two societies, it is difficult to imagine Anglicanism having a significant presence in the colonies.

The Great Awakening of the 1740s

As a religious movement, the Great Awakening advanced renewal, revival, and personal conversion. Churches that welcomed the awakened—like the Presbyterians, Baptists, and certain branches of Congregationalism—experienced rapid growth. For the first time, Christianity also began to significantly engage African Americans.

Figure 20　Whitefield preaching to huge crowds during his preaching tours in colonial America.

By and large, Anglicans were unimpressed, even though Anglican priest **George Whitefield** was the foremost preacher of the Great Awakening. Anglicans tended to emphasize rationalism, as opposed to "enthusiasm" and personal expression. Likewise, the prayer book provided a structured liturgy, as opposed to "alternative" worship like preaching services and revival meetings held throughout the week. In other words, Anglican understandings of faith didn't mix well with the awakened masses.

The Absence of Bishops

You may be surprised to learn there was no bishop in the American colonies for the entirety of their existence (1607–1784). The simple truth is, there was no precedent or provision for extending English church structures beyond England. Bishops also had clearly defined legal as well as ecclesial functions, sat in the House of Lords, and had authority over certain aspects of marriage and inheritance. How could such a system transplant to the haphazard patchwork colonies? Without a clear path for creating or appointing local bishops, the colonies went without. As a result, colonial Anglicanism provides a 177-year experiment with a congregational, non-episcopal, prayer book–based form of Anglicanism.

The American Revolution and the Establishment of the Episcopal Church

What happens to the Church of England when revolutionaries drive the English out of power? One word: devastation. Up to 50 percent of Anglican laypeople and clergy fled to Canada, England or elsewhere. Vandals attacked Anglican churches and sometimes they attacked Anglicans themselves. The rector of Christ Church in Rye, New York, was murdered, likely because of his Tory sympathies (he refused to leave out prayers for the king).

With the cessation of hostilities in 1781, the shattered group of Anglicans who were left began to organize. What would it mean to belong to a nation that was independent from England? How could they provide for clergy with no bishops and no opportunity to travel to England to seek ordination? Once again, they adopted different strategies in different regions.

Anglicans in the mid-Atlantic colonies met at the state level to chart a course for the church. **William White**, a prominent priest in Philadelphia, introduced a plan in his 1782 pamphlet, *The Case of the Episcopal Churches, Considered.* He called for the Church to be organized in each state, with elected "superintendents" with the administrative functions of a bishop. White acknowledged the necessity of securing a bishop for the new church, but also knew negotiations between the colonies and England could drag on for years.

In response to the initiatives of the middle colonies, the church in Connecticut took forceful action. Ten clergymen met in Connecticut and elected **Samuel Seabury** to seek consecration as a bishop in England. Unable to convince the English authorities, he secured episcopal consecration from Scotland in return for a promise to use the Scottish eucharistic prayer in the liturgy.

Church conventions met in 1785 and 1786, without Seabury and the New England churches. Those conventions drafted a constitution and a prayer book for the new church, which was called the **Protestant Episcopal Church in the United States of America**. In the meantime, Parliament amended its laws, and the way was cleared for William White and Samuel Provoost to be ordained bishops in 1787.

Someone had to unite these diverging strands. In 1789, **General Convention** crafted a compromise to unite the New England churches and the new Protestant Episcopal Church. A House of Bishops was proposed in addition to a House of Deputies with clergy and lay representation. Seabury's consecration was recognized as valid. Leaders also made several changes to the proposed prayer book of 1785.

It took time, but the disparate strands came together to form the Episcopal Church. It was Anglicanism, but an Anglicanism unlike the Church of England: bishops were elected, laity had an equal say in church governance, the prayer book was an adapted form of the 1662 Prayer Book of the Church of England, and it was not supported through any state taxes.

It was Anglicanism, adapted, and it was American. But would it survive?

The Church Convalescent: 1789–1835

One of the histories of the Episcopal Church refers to the fifty years after 1789 as "the church convalescent," given the challenges Anglicanism faced in the wake of the American Revolution. What did the Episcopal Church look like in its first decades?

For one thing, the episcopacy looked very different. Most bishops had a day job; they were by and large rectors of congregations who performed episcopal duties like ordaining and confirming on the side. There also weren't many of them. In 1790, there were four bishops. In 1810, there were still only six. General Convention struggled to collect representation from across the new church. The 1789 General Convention that formed the Episcopal Church was attended by two bishops, twenty clergy, and sixteen laypersons. More than twenty years later, two bishops, twenty-five clergy, and twenty laypersons attended the 1811 General Convention.

In Virginia, the heartland of Anglicanism in the eighteenth century, the Church had withered on the vine. In 1807 only fifteen clergy attended the Diocesan Convention, the governing body for the diocese. They didn't bother holding another one until 1812. In New England, home to dozens of Society for the Propagation of the Gospel missionaries in the eighteenth century, the number of functioning churches was so low that all the states, with the exception of Connecticut, merged into a single diocese.

The Episcopal Church grew slowly but steadily, nowhere near the phenomenal pace of other denominations. Imagine it: In the late 1770s, there were maybe ten to fifteen thousand members of Methodist societies, while some estimates were that Anglicans claimed 15–20 percent of the population as a whole, in the hundreds of thousands. In 1812, by contrast, there were one hundred sixty thousand Methodists spread into the new states across the Alleghenies, compared to a paltry fifteen thousand Episcopalians, situated almost entirely on the East Coast.

Turning the Tide

Two particular factors helped the Episcopal Church to move toward real growth. One was a series of bishops who, well, acted like bishops. **John Henry Hobart** (1811–1830) was instrumental in expanding the church in New York State. He traveled tirelessly, performed confirmations and ordinations, and established new parishes. The number of clergy in the diocese increased from twenty-six to 133 in his tenure, and so many parishes were founded that the diocese of New York (originally the entire state) was the first to divide into two dioceses because of growth.

Richard Channing Moore, second bishop of Virginia, oversaw the founding of Virginia Seminary, served as bishop for nearly thirty years, and increased the number of clergy from fourteen to 170.

Bishops didn't make all the difference. The Church radically reimagined how it understood itself, and began to commit, as a whole, to spreading the good news. For some time, Episcopalians simply weren't interested in actively expanding to new areas and building new churches. William White, bishop of Pennsylvania, did not visit the western part of the diocese until the 1820s, after he had been bishop for nearly thirty years.

These attitudes began to change in the 1820s. The **Domestic and Foreign Missionary Society (DFMS)** was founded in 1821 to support missionary work. A membership-based organization, it raised funds through individual dues. Too few people joined, so they didn't raise much money. In 1835, the General Convention changed the DFMS charter. Rather than people joining as individuals, the entire church was declared a missionary society, and everyone, by virtue of their baptism, was a member.

The 1835 General Convention also passed legislation permitting the election of missionary bishops. This allowed the Church to become proactive in missionary work, electing bishops to go forth to plant congregations and organize dioceses.

Anglicanism had transplanted itself to a foreign context almost by accident. By the nineteenth century, the Episcopal Church had proved it could not only survive but even begin to thrive.

Chapter 10

Modernity's Challenge:
The Early Episcopal Church

In the eighteenth and nineteenth centuries, religion was under siege. Thanks to the intellectual movement collectively known as **the Enlightenment**, advances in science and philosophy were casting doubt on Christianity's uniqueness (to say nothing of its veracity). Geology directly challenged biblical authority, since scientists could now prove the earth was older than the Bible claimed, and that flood waters never covered the planet.

Other Protestant denominations held heresy trials and even split over the authority of the Bible and the influx of new ideas and learning. Anglicans and Episcopalians responded to the challenge of modernity in several ways.

Look Back to Go Forward: The Oxford Movement

If you attend an Episcopal church on Sunday, look around. Do you see a priest wearing a stole? Liturgical colors appropriate to the season? A choir that processes into the church and wears surplices? The celebration of saints and other liturgical holidays? The occasional whiff of incense?

In the year 1830, an Anglican of most any stripe would have been shocked, horrified, and likely enraged by those practices. All are the result of the Oxford Movement, the single most important shift in Anglicanism in the last two hundred years, profoundly influencing doctrine, liturgy, and ecclesiology.

The Movement Begins

The Oxford Movement emerged from a European and American cultural phenomenon known as **Romanticism**. Where the Enlightenment emphasized the collective, reason, science, rational thought, and the future, the Romantic Movement did just the opposite. It focused on beauty, transcendence, and the mysterious, with a deep longing for the past, particularly the medieval period.

It was when the Romantic spirit mixed with politics that the Oxford Movement came to life. Trouble started because of a strategy to reduce the number of dioceses in the (Anglican) Church of Ireland, take the savings, and augment church salaries for poorer clergy. **John Keble**, a professor at Oxford, reacted strongly against this proposal and preached a sermon called "The National Apostasy." He rallied several local rectors and Oxford professors, all of whom worried over the undue interference of the state in the life of the church. After all, the church was an apostolic institution, established by Christ and bearing the faith of the apostles. The state had no right to meddle.

So they published a series of pamphlets that became known as the **Tracts for the Times**. They highlighted the role of bishops as successors of the apostles and argued for a higher doctrine of the Eucharist, a greater sense of the ministry as a sacred calling, the role of worship as the infusion of sacramental grace, and celebrating the liturgical calendar.

Keble eventually passed the baton to biblical scholar Edward Pusey and **John Henry Newman**, the greatest mind of the movement. Newman eventually began to think that Anglicanism, instead of being the "middle way" between Protestantism and Catholicism, had departed from Catholic doctrine. He retired from an active role in the Oxford Movement, and eventually departed for the Roman Catholic Church in 1845. He later became a cardinal and even now is on the path toward sainthood.

The Movement Spreads

After Newman's departure, the movement took on new life outside the university. The second generation of leaders applied the principles of the movement to innovative liturgy, hymnody, and church architecture. Churches began holding communion weekly and then daily. Altar rails appeared; the sacrament was reserved; confession was introduced; the ringing of bells and elevation of the elements practiced. Religious orders were formed for the first time since the sixteenth century.

Needless to say, the Oxford Movement met with substantial resistance. The so-called "surplice riots" resulted from groups outraged at a clergy who dared to preach wearing a surplice instead of a black gown. Despite initial resistance, many critics were silenced by the sacrificial and transformative work of several Oxford priests in inner city or "slum" parishes.

Oxford Comes to America

The Oxford Movement flowed to the Episcopal Church in the early 1840s. Here many of the movement's supporters threw their

Figure 21 A depiction of the so-called "surplice riots," protests against liturgical changes.

energy into mission work. Several were elected missionary bishops, and **Nashotah House** was founded as a religious community on what was then the frontier in 1842 and became a seminary of the Episcopal Church. As in England, the upholders of the Oxford Movement also met with great resistance, including a heresy investigation at the General Theological Seminary in New York City.

Matters came to a head in the 1870s, when passionate debates erupted at General Convention about whether ritual practices like use of incense, crucifixes in church, and bowing at the altar were acceptable. There was no formal condemnation, and the way was paved for those elements to become the norm within a century.

An Enlightened Church

Not all Anglicans chose to reject modernity and Enlightenment wisdom. Many drew on the authority of Scripture, Tradition, and Reason to incorporate new learnings and biblical criticism into the faith and witness of the Church. We see this flexibility in two publications: *Essays and Reviews* (1860) and *Lux Mundi* (1889).

- *Essays and Reviews* collected essays by prominent young scholars of the Church of England. Of particular interest was **Benjamin Jowett**'s contribution. A professor of Greek at Oxford, he argued that the Old Testament had too many contradictions to be taken literally, and that the Bible should be read like any other book. The collection kicked up such a firestorm that eventually it was censured on both sides of the Atlantic, but not before it helped shift a generation's attitude toward the Bible and science.

- *Lux Mundi* came out in 1889. Under the leadership of **Charles Gore**—professor at Oxford and later bishop—this collection of essays on the Incarnation managed to weave together the spirit of Anglo-Catholicism and evolving thinking about Christ's humanity and divinity.

New Life: The Evangelical Revival

Other Anglicans and Episcopalians embraced a different course, forgoing the Enlightenment for an Awakening.

That movement owes much of its life to the witness of **John Wesley**. While at Oxford University, Wesley, a faithful Anglican, took part in a group that practiced prayer, fasting, small group Bible study, and weekly communion. In 1738, after a failed attempt as a missionary in Georgia, Wesley experienced a conversion experience and felt his heart "strangely warmed" and was convinced that Jesus had died for him.

This marked an important piece of the evangelical revival: the personal feeling of God's grace in one's life. As his comrade George Whitefield spread that message in the colonies, Wesley traveled up and down the British Isles, preaching thousands of sermons. He encouraged his followers to meet for prayer, to listen to preaching by authorized laypersons, and to attend weekly services at the local Anglican parish.

Meanwhile, John's brother **Charles Wesley** wrote popular and beloved hymns that you're likely to hear today in churches of every kind. Prior to this time most Anglican churches probably sang very few hymns, and even those were Psalms adapted for chanting or singing. Hymnody gave leaders a new way to express the theology of the evangelical revival. Think of the personal relationship

Figure 22 Wesley was refused permission to preach where his father had been rector, so he preached from atop his father's tombstone in the church graveyard.

and yearning evident in the song "Amazing Grace": "how sweet the sound that saved a wretch like me"; "'twas grace that brought me safe thus far, and grace will lead me home."

Evangelicals readily turned their interest beyond personal salvation and toward social causes. Led by leaders like **William Wilberforce**, the evangelical party took a passionate interest in eradicating the slave trade in the British Empire. Women were often on the frontlines of these evangelical ministries. Wesley allowed them as lay preachers, and women like **Hannah Moore** helped to establish Sunday schools (an effort to provide low-cost education to children) and advocated against the slave trade. Despite initial resistance, by the year 1800 the evangelicals were a significant force in the Church of England.

The evangelical revival in the Episcopal Church must be placed within the continuum of American religious history. In the early 1800s the nation witnessed a **Second Great Awakening**. With the opening of the frontier, settlers and missionaries streamed over the Appalachian Mountains into the Midwest and South. Travelling preachers and revivals passed through these frontier towns, and most denominations across America experienced rapid growth. While it had a significant evangelical party that emphasized individual conversion, preaching, and Bible study, evangelicalism in the Episcopal Church was rarely marked with the revivalism and itinerant preaching of other denominations.

Many evangelicals in the Episcopal Church also refused to take up the English evangelical cry against slavery. The Episcopal Church was of decidedly mixed opinion on the question: it contained both ardent abolitionists, such as the Jay family (including John Jay, first attorney general of the United States), and significant numbers of slaveholders, along with those who may not have liked slavery, but accepted it as the law of the land. The church's leaders, including evangelicals, preferred not to rock the boat.

Chapter 11

A Church with a Mission:

The Nineteenth-Century Episcopal Church

The nineteenth century presented the still new Episcopal Church with a host of opportunities to expand relationships beyond the white, rational elite who comprised its leadership. How did the Church respond? As is we have seen, in decidedly both/and manner.

Mission at Home: African American Engagement

In the last chapter, we witnessed Episcopal evangelical ambivalence regarding slavery. That ambivalence ran churchwide and bone-deep.

In general, churches were unclear whether baptism changed the status of a slave. Wouldn't it imply equality before God? To be safe, Anglican missionaries introduced an additional question into the baptismal rite for slaves, asking them to affirm that they were not seeking baptism for any reasons related to freedom or emancipation.

With the way cleared, Southern Episcopalians made a valiant effort to evangelize among slaves, highlighting biblical passages like Ephesians 6 or Colossians 3 that urged servants to obey their masters. Episcopalians were also wary of seeing African Americans converted by the evangelistic preaching of Baptists and Methodists. Southern Episcopal churches often built a slave chapel for separate worship, or seated slaves in the gallery of the local church. Due to these efforts, by the Civil War, a significant proportion of communicants in some dioceses were slaves, particularly in Virginia and South Carolina.

In the North, blacks had more options. For some time, Richard Allen and **Absalom Jones** attended and led a large, separate black worship group through St. George's Methodist Episcopal Church in Philadelphia. One Sunday, they attempted to pray at the church's altar rail and were literally pulled off their knees and told to sit in the gallery. Jones, Allen, and others walked out and in 1787 founded the Free African Society in Philadelphia.

Eventually Jones organized **St. Thomas African Episcopal Church**, which was received into the Diocese of Pennsylvania in 1794. The Diocese agreed to let St. Thomas Church have its own priest and control its own affairs, though it took nearly ten years to

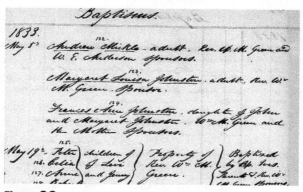

Figure 23 Church register recording baptisms of enslaved Africans.

ordain Jones a priest. The church was also admitted into the Diocese, on the condition that St. Thomas have neither voice nor vote.

The St. Thomas's pattern repeated in cities like New York, New Haven, Detroit, and Baltimore, where African Americans formed congregations, got local control, and submitted candidates for ordination, but they were denied voice and vote.

Ambivalence in the Face of Crisis

The Episcopal Church was eager to pursue the path of least conflict with regard to African Americans and slavery. Unlike many other Protestant denominations, the Episcopal Church theoretically did not split over the issue. This isn't necessarily a source of pride: other churches split because leaders took strong, irreconcilable positions for and against slavery. As we've noted, while some Episcopalians were involved in abolitionism, the Church had more than its share of large slaveholders, as well as people involved in other aspects of the slave trade, such as shipping and finance. In 1861, **John Henry Hopkins**, bishop of Vermont and later presiding bishop, published a defense of slavery on biblical grounds.

While the Church did not split over slavery, it did split over secession. Southern leaders formed their own Protestant Episcopal Church in the Confederate States. The rest of the Church turned a blind eye, and the 1862 General Convention roll call started with Alabama. After the war, the southern dioceses were reintegrated into General Convention.

The welcome mat provided to Southern churches after the war never quite extended to African Americans. A pattern of separate but equal quickly prevailed throughout the Church. In 1883, leaders considered a proposal to create a non-geographic diocese to encompass black churches. While never enacted, a version of this segregationist proposal was made at every General Convention until 1940. In addition, African Americans were routinely denied admission to seminaries in the North, where churches were just as likely to be racially segregated.

The Church's record on African American engagement is mixed at best. On the one hand, **Henry Beard Delany**, the first African American elected a bishop, was born a slave. Yet Delany and other black leaders ministered in a church that refused to challenge slavery or segregation for much of its history.

Missions from Sea to Shining Sea

In one way the history of Christianity *is* the history of mission. It's glorious to imagine: a bunch of Galilean fishermen and a combative former Pharisee (Paul) changed the world. Yet mission work has often involved cultural, racial and economic oppression, as well as Christian triumphalism, colonialism, and paternalism. The **Doctrine of Discovery** is a perfect case; originated under King Henry VII in 1496, it gave Christian leaders the right to assert dominion over any lands they "discovered," with the Church's blessing. (The Episcopal Church voted to repudiate the doctrine in 2012.)

The 1800s saw a tremendous expansion of both American and English presence throughout the world, especially in Africa and Asia. New missionary organizations formed to manage all this activity. The evangelical revival in England formed the **Church Missionary Society (CMS)**. As the nineteenth century proceeded, the CMS developed a strong evangelical bent, and the high-church and Anglo-Catholic bishops eventually dominated the Society for the Propagation of the Gospel.

American and English political presence often went hand-in-hand with missionary work, but not always. In some places, such as West Africa and Nigeria, missionaries preceded England's imperial ambitions; in 1864, they consecrated the first African Anglican bishop, **Samuel Ajayi Crowther**. In other places, the cross and the crown arrived together: after the Spanish-American War, when the Philippines became an American colony, the same ship that brought the appointed governor also brought a missionary

Figure 24 Samuel Ajayi Crowther, first person of African descent consecrated bishop in the Anglican Communion.

bishop. In other places, missionaries actively spoke against the abuses of imperialism and colonialism.

Missionary Strategies

The CMS pioneered the so-called **three-self missionary strategy**: to create churches that were self-supporting (financially), self-governing, and self-propagating, with an emphasis on training teachers and evangelists to do missionary work and preparing local, "native" clergy as quickly as possible.

The missionary bishop model came to dominate Episcopal domestic missions. The Church adopted a missionary bishops' canon in 1835, which allowed it to commission leaders like **Jackson Kemper** to organize the church in what is now Wisconsin, Iowa, Missouri, and other parts of the West. Religious orders born in the Anglo-Catholic revival poured energy into missionary work. The Society of St. John the Evangelist established congregations in the United States and had missionary houses as far away as Japan.

The task of a missionary bishop was often overwhelming: Bishop William Kip oversaw the whole state of California, quite a feat in 1850 with no transportation infrastructure. Bishop Daniel Tuttle managed a missionary diocese that covered Idaho, Montana, and Utah. By 1900, The Episcopal Church stretched from coast to coast and included missionary endeavors in China, the Philippines, and Africa. Despite this expansion, the Church remained largely an urban, East Coast movement: in 1900, 90 percent of Episcopalians lived east of the Mississippi.

Missionary Work and Role of Women

Just as women played key roles in the evangelical revival, they regularly took the lead in missions and in frontier congregations. Men often worked long hours in factories, mines, ranches, or banks, and women handled plenty of the day-to-day workings of the church, especially fundraising.

After the Civil War, Episcopal women formed a number of organizations devoted to issues like temperance and missions. The most important was the **Women's Auxiliary to the Board of Missions**. The Women's Auxiliary raised money and collected supplies for missionaries and, under the leadership first of **Mary Emery** (national secretary from 1871–1876) and then her sister **Julia Emery** (national secretary from 1876–1916), the Auxiliary became a driving force in the Church's mission work. They formed a network of local representatives spread throughout parishes and dioceses, and by 1900 these powerful women were raising a huge chunk of the Board of Missions' budget.

While the Board welcomed their money, Julia Emery had to lobby consistently for women's representation on the Board of Missions. Later the Women's Auxiliary morphed into the **Episcopal Church Women (ECW)**, and their fundraising effort came to be known as the United Thank Offering.

Women funded ministry, but they also engaged in hands-on ministry, both via the growing number of women's religious orders and the office of deaconess. This allowed lots of women to work full-time in church ministry, largely in education and social service.

The Episcopal Church and the Labor Movement

Social ministries were more necessary than ever by the nineteenth century. Keep in mind the massive scale of industrialization and urbanization: Chicago had perhaps five thousand people in 1840; by 1900, it had 1.7 million, many of whom worked in deplorable conditions and lived in slums. Some of the wealthiest barons of the Industrial Revolution sat in Episcopal pews (and built Episcopal churches), but Episcopal leaders continued to step out for social ministry and justice.

Anglican priest **Frederick Dennison Maurice** (d. 1872) grounded this work in a clear theology of social justice. In *The Kingdom of Christ*, he argued that Christ came to found a kingdom: the kingdom of God. But Maurice did more than write. He helped to start workers' cooperatives and to launch the Christian Socialism movement in order to apply Christian principles and values to all parts of life, including economics.

Leaders like **Vida Scudder** brought that ministry to life in America. One of the first American women to graduate from Oxford, Scudder understood privilege. Yet, as a professor at Wellesley College in Massachusetts, she was devoted to the Society of Companions of the Holy Cross, a community of laywomen united in study and prayer for justice. She wrote prolifically on matters of faith and justice, spoke in support of striking textile workers, organized with the Christian Social Union, and led the establishment of Denison House, a Boston settlement house where middle-class laypeople lived and worked alongside the immigrants and poor people receiving housing, job training, and education.

In 1887, Episcopalians founded the **Church Association for the Advancement of the Interests of Labor**, better known as

CAIL. With the support of a number of bishops and numerous local chapters, CAIL worked to improve working conditions, to shorten the workday and workweek, and to arbitrate between unions and management in a time when strikebreaking and labor violence was all too common.

Nineteenth century social developments forced Anglicans in England and America to put their faith into action. The twentieth century, in turn, presented the Church with similar challenges, but against the backdrop of an increasingly rapidly changing world.

Chapter 12

History in the Making:

The Episcopal Church and Anglican Communion in the Twentieth Century

We now enter treacherous territory: writing the history of the [more] recent past. This can be tricky because perspective so often shapes how we view the past. Harry Truman left office with some of the lowest approval ratings for any president, yet in hindsight historians often consider him an excellent president. Events or people that seem important now may be less so in centuries to come, and those we overlook today may stand out later.

The Pre–World War II Church

The period from 1919–1945 in many ways marks the dawn of the modern Episcopal Church. The 1919 General Convention, in particular, laid the foundations for many of the organizational structures and systems that shaped the Church in the twentieth century:

1. **Full-time elected presiding bishop**: Prior to 1919, the presiding bishop was simply the senior bishop, and the major job was presiding over the House of Bishops every three years and handling disciplinary proceedings against bishops.

That made sense for the decentralized church of the 1700s. As the Church grew larger and more complex, the presiding bishop needed to provide more leadership and cohesion and increasingly to function as primate and chief pastor.

2. **Organized structures for mission**: There was not much "denominational" infrastructure apart from the General Convention and some ad hoc committees or groups gathering for various causes. The 1919 Convention established the National Council (later **Executive Council**), which had two functions: to run the church in between General Conventions, and to take charge of the mission work of the church.

The **Ecumenical Movement** also took root in this period, and the Episcopal Church played a crucial role. In 1910, most of the Protestant churches gathered for the World Missionary Conference in Edinburgh, Scotland. Their goal: to avoid confrontation and competition in the foreign mission field and to collaborate on spreading the gospel. Bishop **Charles Henry Brent** (senior chaplain to U.S. forces in World War I) attended on behalf of the Episcopal Church, and a young William Temple (later archbishop of Canterbury) attended from the Church of England. Their work

Figure 25 Bishop Brent on the cover of *Time* magazine, 1927.

set in motion the process that led to the establishment of the World Council of Churches in 1948.

The Church and the Civil Rights Movement

Events that shaped American life after World War II also made their mark on the Episcopal Church. Episcopalians stood on both sides of the struggle for civil rights in America. The 1955 General Convention was moved to Honolulu when the original location, Houston, was unable to provide equal accommodations for people of color. In 1959 the **Episcopal Society for Cultural and Racial Unity** was formed, with African American and white Episcopalians working side-by-side for freedom. In 1964, the General Convention officially banned racial discrimination in churches. And in 1965, **Jonathan Myrick Daniels**, a seminarian from the Episcopal Theological School in Cambridge, was working as a volunteer when he was gunned down in Alabama (and whose murderer was acquitted by an all-white jury).

As always, the story has its share of complications. Even some of the "setbacks" led the Church forward: in 1952 the Board of Trustees of the School of Theology at Sewanee voted not to admit African American students. When half the faculty and more than half the students either resigned or transferred in protest, the Board reconsidered and voted to integrate. Separate but equal in theological education eroded in the 1950s, as African American students began to enter predominantly white seminaries, and the historically black Bishop Payne Seminary merged with Virginia Theological Seminary.

The Church took its most dramatic steps forward in 1967, when Presiding Bishop John Hines challenged Episcopalians to respond to the needs of inner cities and historically underprivileged groups. The Convention established the General Convention Special Program (GCSP) and allocated $3 million toward it in the 1967–1970 triennium.

Some grants proved controversial, and the furor rose so high that for only the second time in the history of the Episcopal

Church, a Special Convention was called in 1969 in South Bend, Indiana. The convention was extraordinarily charged, especially with the publication of the Black Manifesto and its call for reparations for slavery. Some black clergy walked out over the way the issue was handled. The GCSP continued after the 1969 Special Convention, but was eventually discontinued, marking a step back from the church's engagement with social justice ministries.

Other ethnic voices also rose in the Church's consciousness. Since 1870, Native American Episcopalians from many tribes and communities had gathered in South Dakota for the **Niobrara Convocation**. These annual gatherings took on additional significance when the Missionary District of Niobrara became the Diocese of South Dakota in 1971.

The churchwide staff also added positions to coordinate mission and ministry with Hispanic/Latino, African American, Asian and Asian American, and Native American Episcopalians, a wise move considering that non–United States communities like the **Diocese of Haiti** would by the twenty-first century become the largest in the Episcopal Church.

Prayer Book Reform

At the height of the Civil Rights Movement, the Church opened the door to liturgical revision. In 1964, prayer book reform was authorized, and two series of experimental rites were issued in 1970 and 1973.

Why change, and why then? Thomas Cranmer's original plan had been Morning Prayer, litany, sermon, and Communion. Some churches held Morning Prayer with an offertory and sermon added. Others held Communion with no Old Testament lesson or Psalm (since, in Cranmer's view, they would have been read at Morning Prayer). In the midst of this divergence, scholars had revealed important wisdom about the shape of the liturgy, and liturgical renewal had swept other denominations. Episcopal leaders decided it was time for the Church to engage, and so it did.

- **Baptism**: Perhaps the most important shift was renewed emphasis on baptism. The new baptismal rite was thoroughly rewritten and placed in the context of the Eucharistic service, rescuing it from its status as a private ceremony performed in a person's home or after the church service. An emphasis on the ministry of the baptized pervades the prayer book. For instance, the ordination rite no longer looked like climbing the ecclesial ladder (the 1928 book famously called the diaconate an "inferior office" through which one passed). Instead, it reflected three distinct offices of ministry, all "ordained" and "consecrated." Persons to be ordained wear a simple white alb symbolic of baptism, instead of the stole or garment indicating their "rank" in the church.

- **Eucharist**: The prayer book also stressed Eucharist as the principle act of worship, and redesigned the rite to reflect newly discovered ancient liturgical texts and practices and to allow for more participation of the laity.

The proposed prayer book passed overwhelmingly in 1976 on a first reading, and in 1979 it became the new liturgy of the church. While some felt the book was not introduced with appropriate pastoral sensitivity and that the 1928 book should have been retained as an alternative, the Church moved forward.

The Ordination of Women

The question of women's ordination also picked up momentum in the 1960s. The order of deaconess declined as the work of teachers, nurses, and social workers became more professionalized.

In 1970, General Convention decided deaconesses differed in no major way from male deacons. The same year a measure to allow for the ordination of women to the priesthood and episcopate was defeated. It came to the floor again in 1973 and garnered significant support, but did not pass.

In 1974, supporters took matters in their own hands and held an ordination service for eleven women deacons in Philadelphia with three retired bishops presiding. The female deacons did not have the consent of their Standing Committees or sponsoring bishops as required in the canons, and the House of Bishops met and declared the ordinations invalid. Some of the priests celebrated communion at the interdenominational Riverside Church in New York City. Tensions ran high. People opposed to women's ordination were angered; some who even supported women's ordination were upset, as they felt the action would polarize the issue even more and risk its passage in 1976. Others felt this was a prophetic action to call the church to stand for justice.

The 1976 Convention met to discuss the matter, and after much debate, the matter passed by a razor-thin majority in the House of Deputies. It also passed in the House of Bishops, but a conscience clause was later adopted by the House of Bishops for those bishops with reservations about ordaining women. This was not officially binding and never submitted to the House of Deputies, and some bishops did not fully open the ordination processes to women.

It's worth noting that, unlike some other provinces of the Communion, the Episcopal Church approved ordination of women to the priesthood *and* the episcopate in 1976. Some other provinces approved women for ordination to the priesthood but not the episcopate. Still, it took another thirteen years before **Barbara Harris** was elected bishop suffragan in the Diocese of Massachusetts in 1989.

Figure 26 Ordinations of eleven women at Church of the Advocate, July 29, 1974, Philadelphia, Pennsylvania.

Human Sexuality

The same convention that approved women's ordination also declared, for the first time, that homosexual people should receive the same care and pastoral reception as heterosexuals. From there, the Church was plunged into a decades-long debate over human sexuality. Bishop **Paul Moore** of New York ordained **Ellen Barrett**, an "openly" lesbian woman, to the priesthood in 1977. The House of Bishops declined to censure Moore, but the 1979 General Convention passed a resolution that declared homosexual behavior (not orientation) and sexual activity outside of marriage to be incompatible with those seeking ordination.

The resolution from 1979 was routinely ignored. Throughout the 1980s many dioceses ordained gay and lesbian persons. The question came to a head in the early 1990s. In 1991 the General Convention debated the matter hotly (metaphorically as well as literally: the convention was in Phoenix in August). Tempers rose and the House of Bishops met in closed session to discuss the matter.

In 1995 Bishop **Walter Righter**, an assisting bishop in Newark, was charged for violating his ordination vows by ordaining a gay man, **Barry Stopfel**, in 1990. The ecclesiastical court ruled that the question of human sexuality was not part of the "core doctrine" of the Episcopal Church, and the charges were dismissed on a procedural motion. The way was effectively clear for the ordination of gay men and lesbians in dioceses that desired to do so.

Another milestone in the debate over human sexuality occurred at the 1998 **Lambeth Conference of Bishops** (the once-every-ten-years gathering of Anglican bishops), which passed resolution I.10, declaring homosexual practice incompatible with Scripture. It's important to remember that Lambeth Conference resolutions are non-binding; however, they do reflect the mind of bishops throughout the Anglican Communion on a given issue. Their mind on this issue was clear: 526 in favor, 70 against, 45 abstaining.

Apart from the matter of human sexuality, one could also argue that Lambeth 1998 was a wake-up call announcing that most of the

Communion differed from the Episcopal Church. It also was the moment many in the Anglican Communion realized the decades-long shift in Christianity, from Europe and related areas like Canada, the United States and Australia to Africa, Asia, and South America.

Matters came to a head in 2003, when the diocese of New Hampshire elected **V. Gene Robinson**, a partnered gay man, as bishop. Since the election happened within a particular window of time, the consents to the election were considered at that summer's General Convention. The required consents were given in the House of Deputies and in the House of Bishops.

This decision set in motion a chain of events that rippled through the Episcopal Church and the Anglican Communion. Eighteen bishops appealed to the archbishop of Canterbury, who set up the panel that drafted the **Windsor Report**, issued in October of 2004. The panel recommended moratoria on consecration of openly gay persons to the episcopate and on the blessing of same sex unions. At the 2005 meeting of the Anglican Consultative Council, the Episcopal Church representatives voluntarily withdrew after being asked to do so by a razor-thin vote of the Council.

The General Convention met in 2006 in Columbus, Ohio, and naturally it considered numerous proposals addressing the Windsor Report. The convention passed a resolution to "call upon Standing Committees and bishops with jurisdiction to exercise restraint by not consenting to the consecration of any candidate to the episcopate whose manner of life presents a challenge to the wider church and will lead to further strains on communion." Conservatives dismissed the compromise; others saw it as a setback to full inclusion. Archbishop of Canterbury Rowan Williams mused that there might be a "two-tier" Anglican Communion.

The convention also elected Bishop **Katharine Jefferts Schori** of Nevada as presiding bishop, making her the first female primate in the Communion (even as the number of female bishops remained fairly stagnant throughout the Church).

The question of blessing same-sex unions has also been regularly discussed in recent years. The 1994 General Convention

Figure 27 Consecration of V. Gene Robinson,
November 2, 2003.

requested a theological report regarding blessing unions other
than marriage, and the matter was addressed at every subsequent
General Convention. In 2012, a rite for blessing same-sex relationships was approved for provisional use, by permission of the
local diocesan bishop. The 2015 General Convention approved
marriage rites and revised the marriage canons accordingly.

Meeting Globalization Again for the First Time

Beginning in the nineteenth century, the global reality of Anglicanism was clear, and leaders realized the need for conversation,
cooperation, and collaboration. The first Lambeth Conference of
Bishops in 1867 gathered bishops from around the Communion.
In the 1960s, additional governing structures were created, including the Anglican Consultative Council, which consists of clergy,
laypersons, and bishops from around the world.

But only recently has Anglicanism—much less the Episcopal Church—begun living into the fullness of being a globalized church, a product of a difficult legacy of imperialism and colonialism.

Look at the two pictures below:

Figure 28 The Lambeth Conference of Bishops, 1867.

Figure 29 The Lambeth Conference of Bishops, 2008.

The first photo is from the 1867 Lambeth Conference. From the 1850s and into the early twentieth century, a whole series of new provinces were created, almost entirely from European areas or areas of European migration: Australia, Ireland, Scotland, Wales, New Zealand, and South Africa, among others.

Through the twentieth century, new provinces were formed in South America, Africa, and Asia, almost entirely in areas with a majority non-European presence. The Church grew in these areas, yet even as late as 1978, the gathering of bishops was largely a white (and all male) gathering of bishops.

The second photo is from the 2008 Lambeth Conference. We can see tremendous growth in the number of bishops and in persons of color— as well as the presence of women bishops. The increase in persons of color is not only a result of newer provinces being formed, but the growth of those provinces in numbers and members. By 2015, there were more than 18 million Anglicans in Nigeria alone, far more than the number of Anglicans practicing in England, Canada, the United States, and Australia combined.

Human sexuality may look like a major fault line, but perhaps it was the presenting issue that revealed massive changes that had already swept over Anglicanism. This major branch of global Christianity could no longer be seen as an extension of English Christianity. But if not that, then what?

Birth and Rebirth

This, I think, will be the main topic of the history of Anglicanism written in 2115: how the twenty-first century birthed a new Anglican synthesis. While I am not inclined toward predictions, this is one I feel most sure about, in part because this has been the story of the last twelve chapters.

Christianity adapts and responds to changes in the world, building on what has brought us thus far, but moving into new ways of being. Christians have always adapted, always been diverse, and always needed to embrace global realities. Anglicanism, from the Reformation to the birth of the Episcopal Church, to the development of the Anglican Communion, has done the same. We can only hope to be as faithful as our forebears, as we are all cocreators of the Christianity that is coming into being.

Suggestions for Further Reading

For the entire history of Christianity up to the present, Diarmaid MacCulloch's *Christianity: The First Three Thousand Years* is an excellent resource. Former Archbishop of Canterbury Rowan Williams, no academic slouch himself, stated that MacCulloch's book has "few, if any, rivals in the English language."

For a good overview of the history of women's experience in the overall development of Christianity, a classic in the field is Barbara MacHaffie's *Her Story: Women in Christian Tradition.*

Part One

Everett Ferguson, *Backgrounds of Early Christianity*

Carter Lindberg, *European Reformations*

Rebecca Lyman, *Early Christian Traditions*

Joseph Lynch, *Early Christianity: A Brief History*

Kevin Madigan, *Medieval Christianity: A New History*

Part Two

Ian Douglas and Kwok Pui-Lan (eds.), *Beyond Colonial Anglicanism*

Christopher Haigh, *English Reformations*

Harold Lewis, *Yet With a Steady Beat: the African-American Struggle for Recognition in the Episcopal Church*

Diarmaid MacCullough, *The Reformation*

Robert Prichard, *A History of The Episcopal Church*

Kevin Ward, *History of Global Anglicanism*

Image Attributions

All images public domain.

Chapter 1

Figure 1: Map of Judea in Jesus' Time (http://www.bibleistrue
.com/qna/israelmap31ad.gif)

Figure 2: War Scroll (http://en.wikipedia.org/wiki/War_of_the
_Sons_of_Light_Against_the_Sons_of_Darkness#/media/
File:The_War_Scroll_-_Dead_Sea_Scroll.jpg)

Chapter 2

Figure 3: Map of Roman Empire, circa 100 CE (https://
en.wikipedia.org/wiki/Roman_province#/media/
File:RomanEmpire_117.svg)

Figure 4: Icon of Justin Martyr (https://www.archangelsbooks
.com/proddetail.asp?prod=HTM-A80)

Figure 5: Nag Hammadi Texts (http://en.wikipedia.org/wiki/
Nag_Hammadi_library#/media/File:NagHammadi_1.jpg)

Chapter 3

Figure 6: Surviving frescoes from the house church in Dura Europos, on the Iraq/Syria border (http://commons.wikimedia.org/wiki/File:Dura_Europos_baptistry_overview.jpg)

Quote: Cyprian of Carthage, *On the Unity of the Church.* Author's translation.

Chapter 4

Figure 7: Constantine presiding over the Council of Nicaea (http://en.wikipedia.org/wiki/Arius#/media/File:Nikea-arius.png)

Quote: Gregory of Nyssa translation from A. D. Lee, *Pagans and Christians in Late Antiquity*, p. 110.

Chapter 5

Figure 8: St Benedict giving his Rule to the monks (http://en.wikipedia.org/wiki/Rule_of_Saint_Benedict#/media/File:St._Benedict_delivering_his_rule_to_the_monks_of_his_order.jpg)

Figure 9: Remains of monastic huts and monastery graveyard, Skellig Michael, off the west coast of Ireland (http://en.wikipedia.org/wiki/Skellig_Michael#/media/File:Skellig_Michael_-_cemetery_and_large_oratory.jpg)

Figure 10: Mosaic of Gregory the Great, Worcester College, Oxford (https://i2.wp.com/farm1.static.flickr.com/159/368941542_cb66c505fc.jpg)

Figure 11: Coronation of Charlemagne by Pope Leo (http://en.wikipedia.org/wiki/Coronation#/media/File:Karel_Leo.jpg)

Chapter 6

Figure 12: Drawing of the abbey of Cluny, eighteenth century
(http://www.oberlin.edu/images/Art335/335-180.JPG)

Figure 13: Christians sacked Constantinople in 1204 instead of
going to the Holy Land (http://en.wikipedia.org/wiki/Fourth_
Crusade#/media/File:Crusaders_attack_Constantinople.jpg)

Chapter 7

Figure 14: Luther defending his beliefs before Charles V at the
Diet of Worms (http://amuseorbemused.com/wp-content/
uploads/2012/10/Diet-of-Worms-Dude.jpg)

Figure 15: Anabaptists punished for rebaptism with execution by
drowning (http://36.media.tumblr.com/14d7f8cb7e782a7da56
995ae4f19faa0/tumblr_mvd8vn4q2J1sykajyo1_1280.jpg)

Chapter 8

Figure 16: Front page of the first official English Bible,
1539 (http://en.wikipedia.org/wiki/Great_Bible#/media/
File:GreatbibleI.jpg)

Figure 17: Elizabeth I presiding over Parliament (https://faculty
.history.wisc.edu/sommerville/361/361-16.htm)

Figure 18: Execution of Charles I, 1649 (http://en.wikipedia
.org/wiki/Charles_I_of_England#/media/File:Contemporary
_German_print_depicting_Charles_Is_beheading.jpg)

Chapter 9

Figure 19: Old Swedes Episcopal Church (https://en.wikipedia
.org/wiki/Holy_Trinity_Church_%28Old_Swedes%29#/
media/File:InteriorOldSwedesHabs.jpg)

Figure 20: Whitefield preaching to huge crowds (http://www
.learnnc.org/lp/multimedia/8804)

Chapter 10

Figure 21: A depiction of the so-called "surplice riots" (http://www.stgite.org.uk/library/riots.jpg)

Figure 22: John Wesley preaching from atop his father's tombstone (http://www.johnandellenduncan.com/jw_grave.htm)

Chapter 11

Figure 23: Church register recording baptisms of enslaved Africans (http://i1.wp.com/prayer.ourstate.com/wp-content/uploads/2013/11/03_lrg_horiz_Graebner_baptism.jpg?resize=767%2C470)

Figure 24: Samuel Ajayi Crowther (http://www.testifynews.com/wp-content/uploads/2014/07/Ajayi-crowther1.jpg)

Chapter 12

Figure 25: Bishop Brent on the cover of *Time* magazine (http://content.time.com/time/covers/0,16641,19270829,00.html)

Figure 26: Ordinations of eleven women (https://dailyoffice.files.wordpress.com/2013/07/philadelphia11-july-29-1974-400.jpg)

Figure 27: Consecration of V. Gene Robinson (http://archive.episcopalchurch.org/images/robinson01_med.jpg)

Figure 28: The Lambeth Conference of Bishops, 1867 (http://www.archbishopofcanterbury.org/data/images/pages/Roles_and_Priorities/Lambeth-Conference-1867.jpg)

Figure 29: The Lambeth Conference of Bishops, 2008 (http://www.anglicancommunion.org/media/99122/2704139372_dec5a245c1_z.jpg